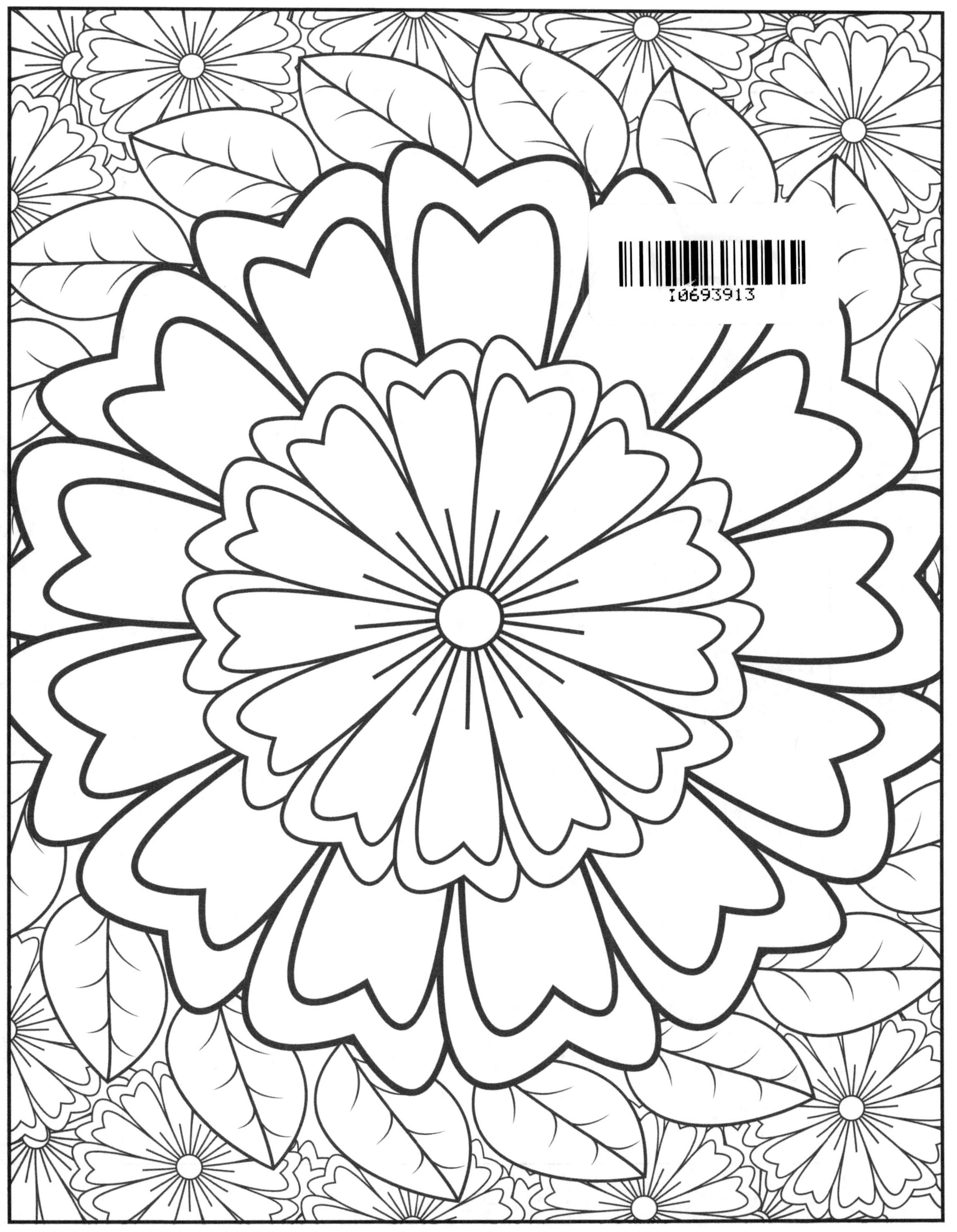
I0693913

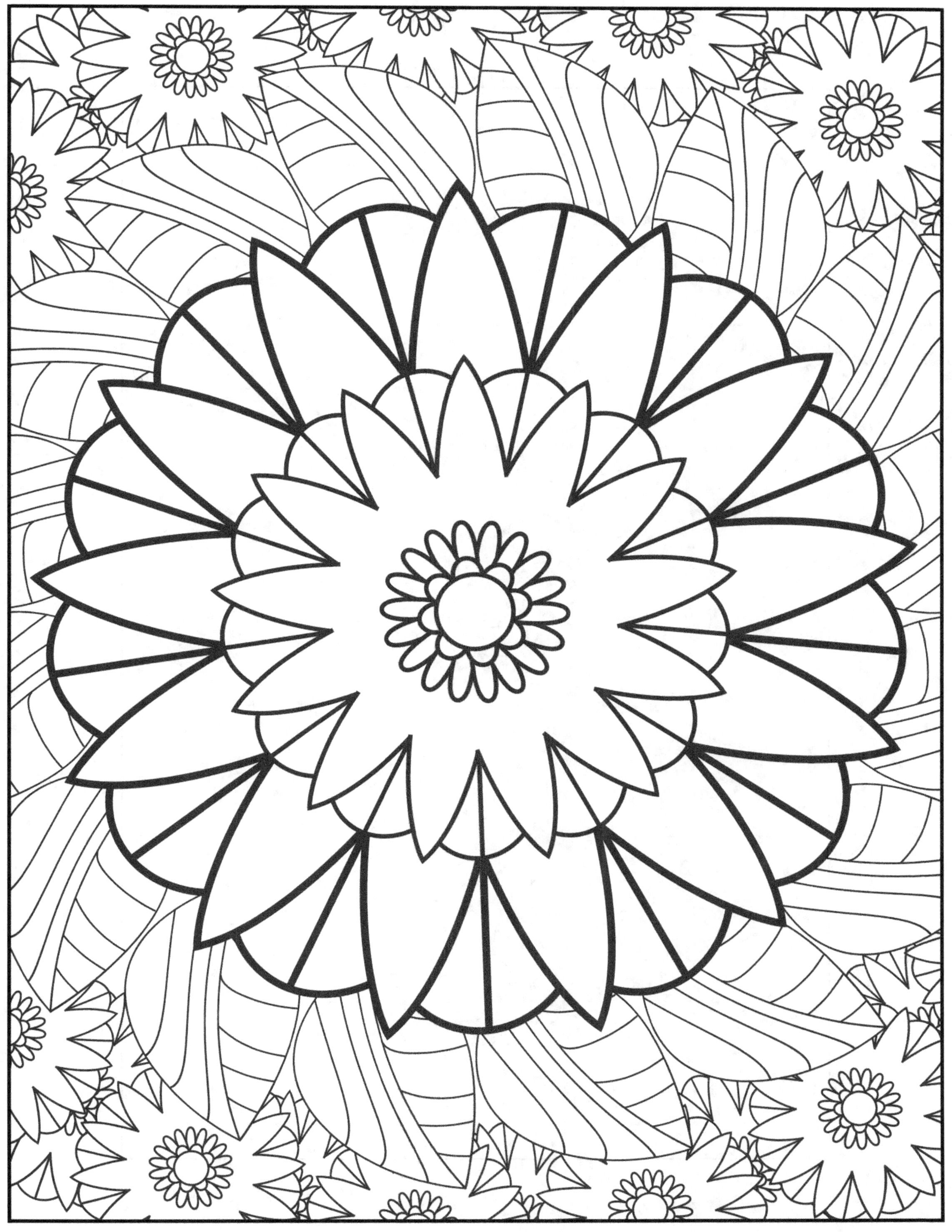

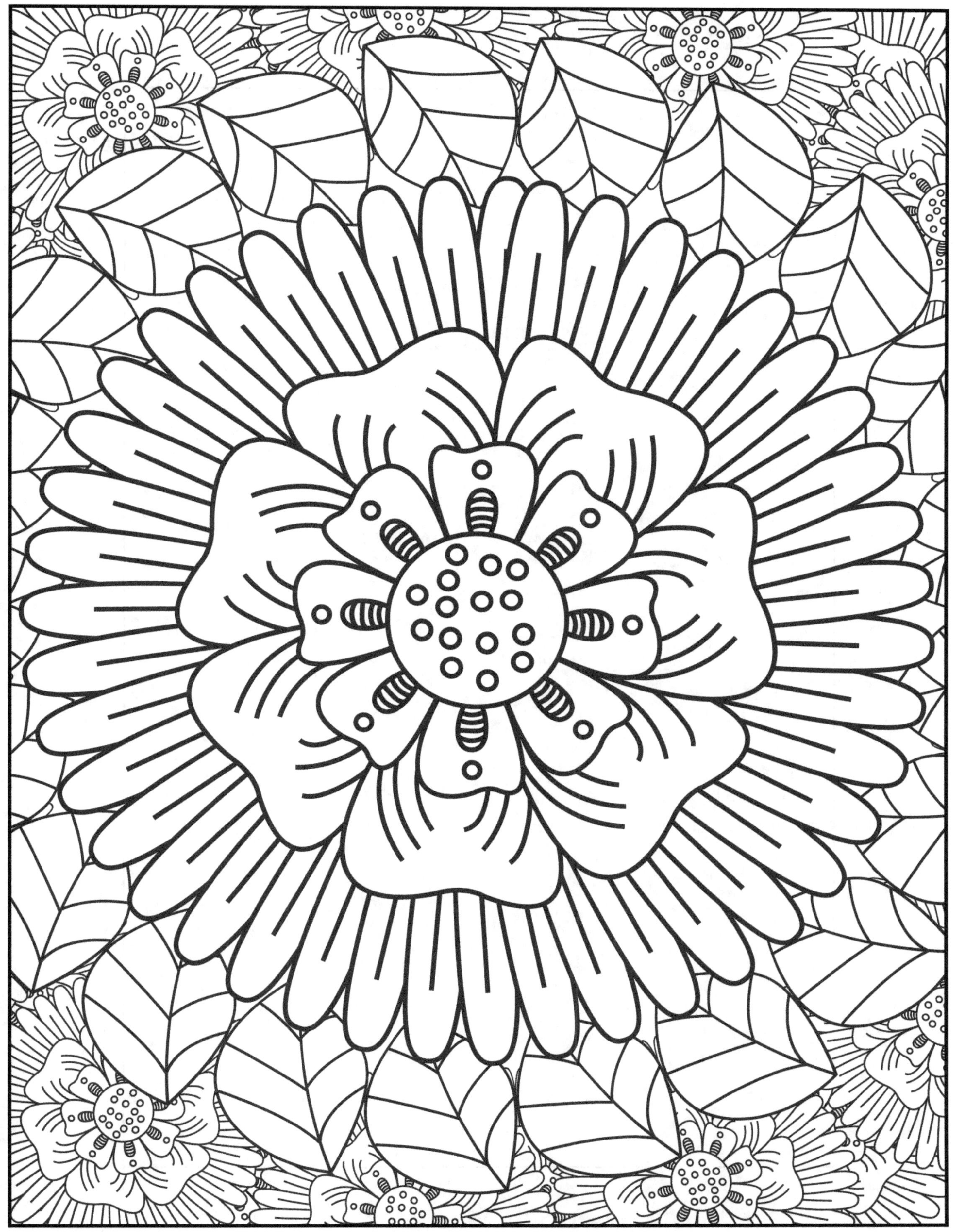

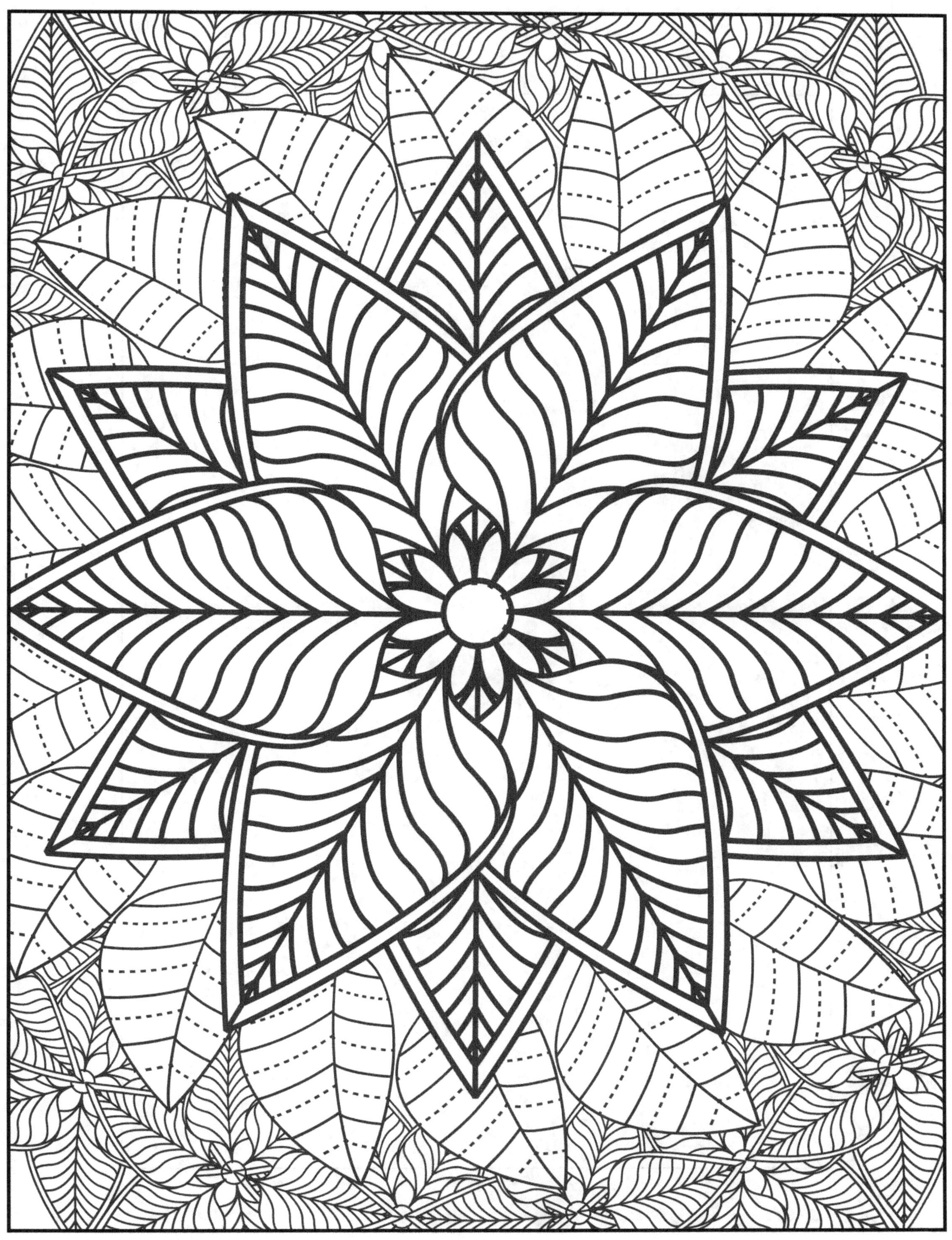

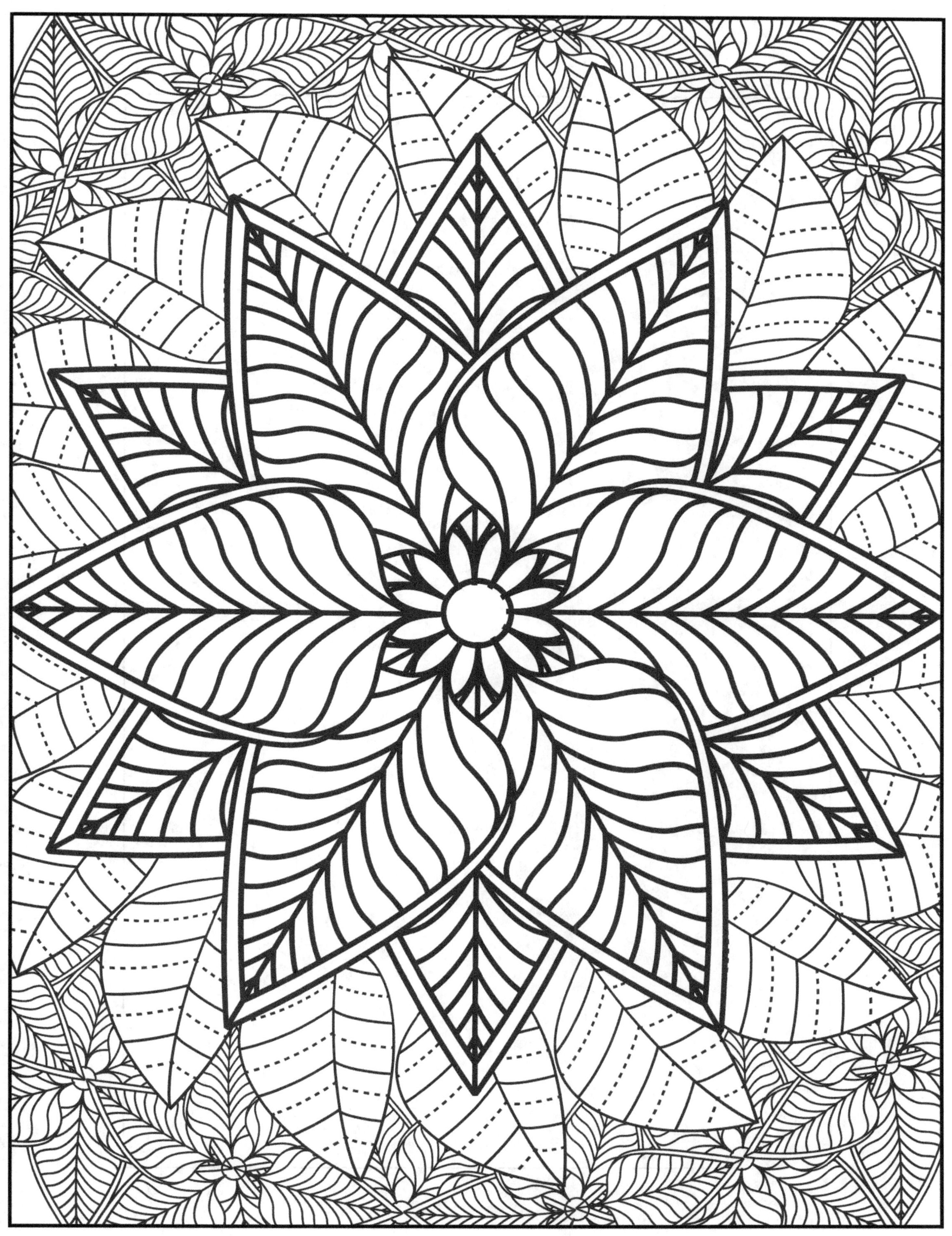

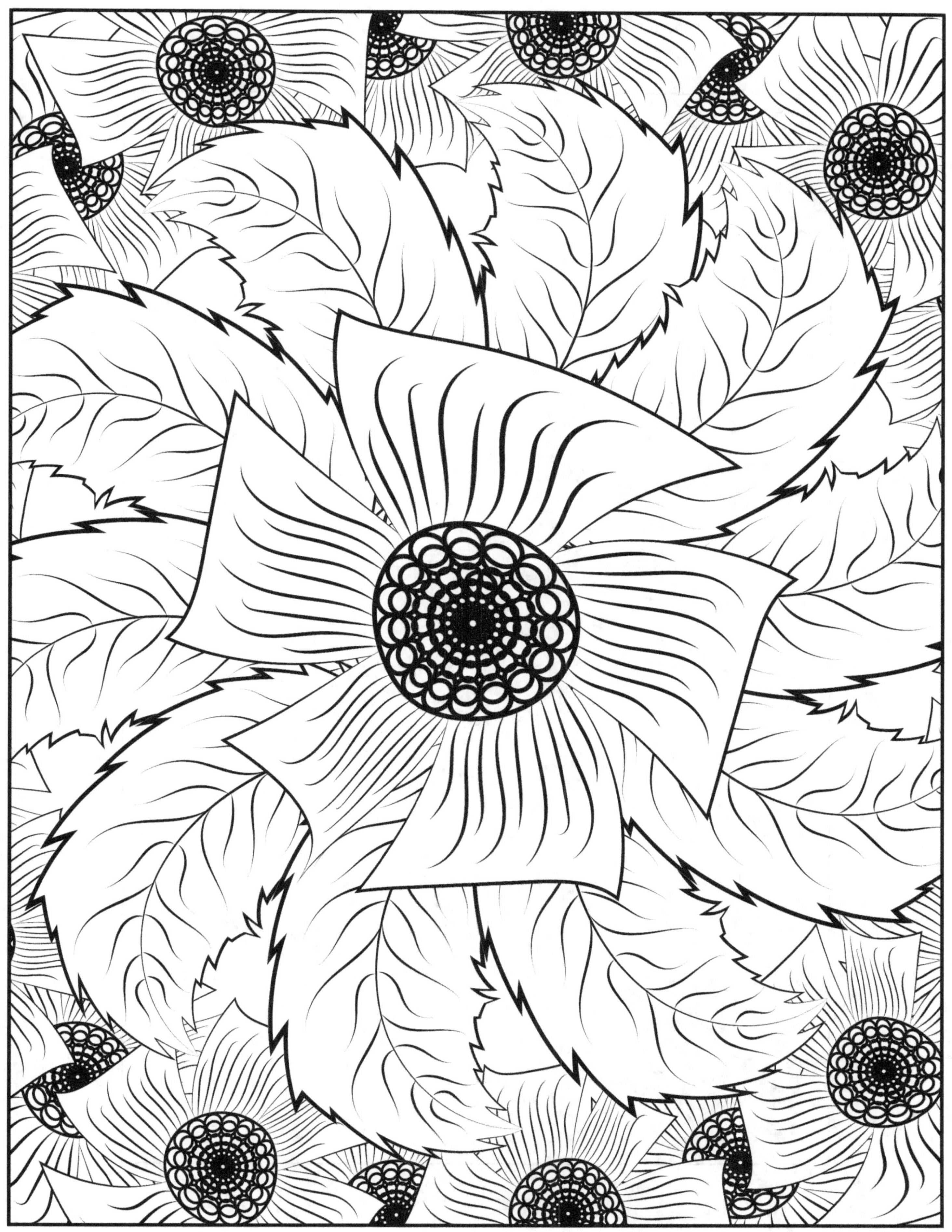

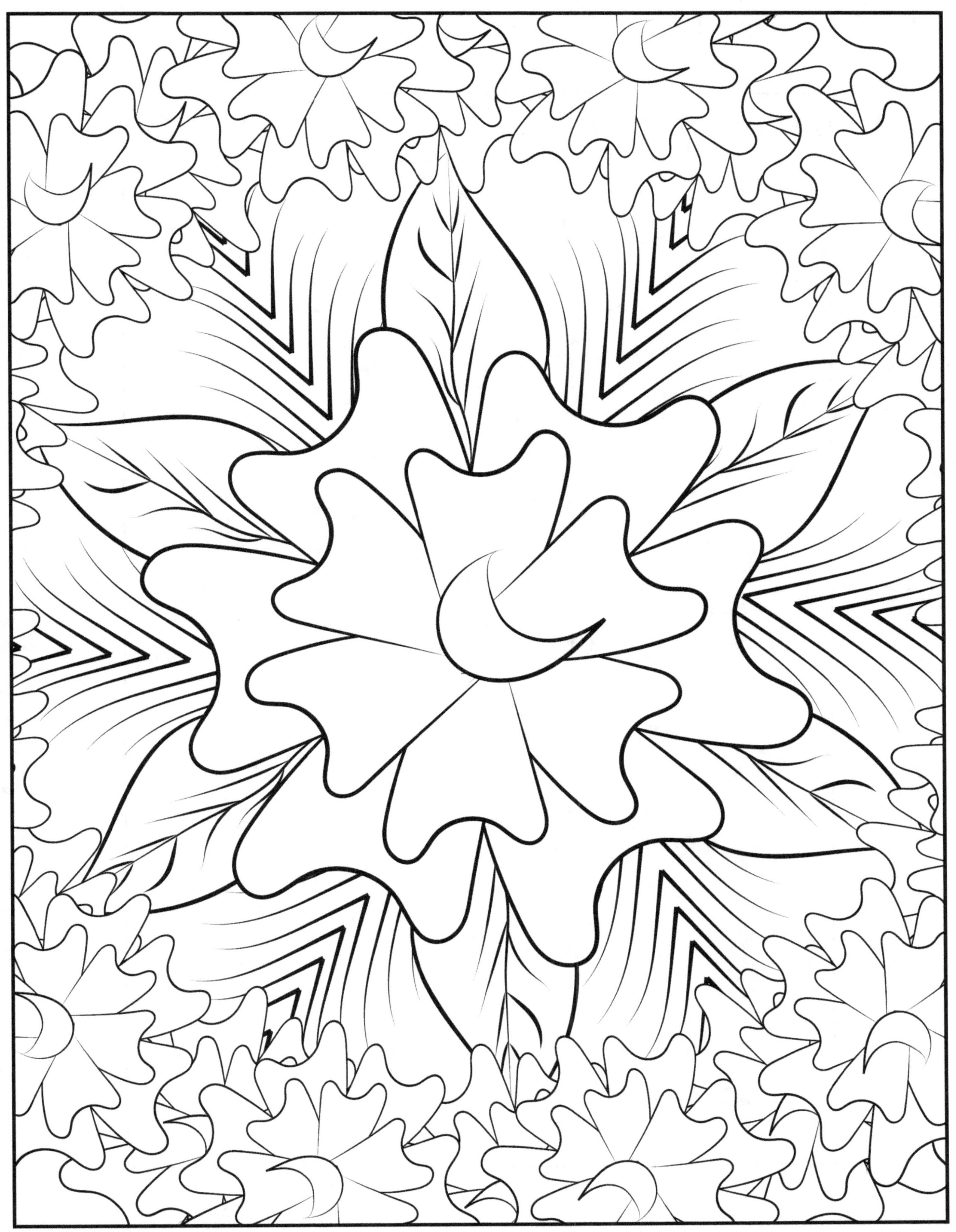

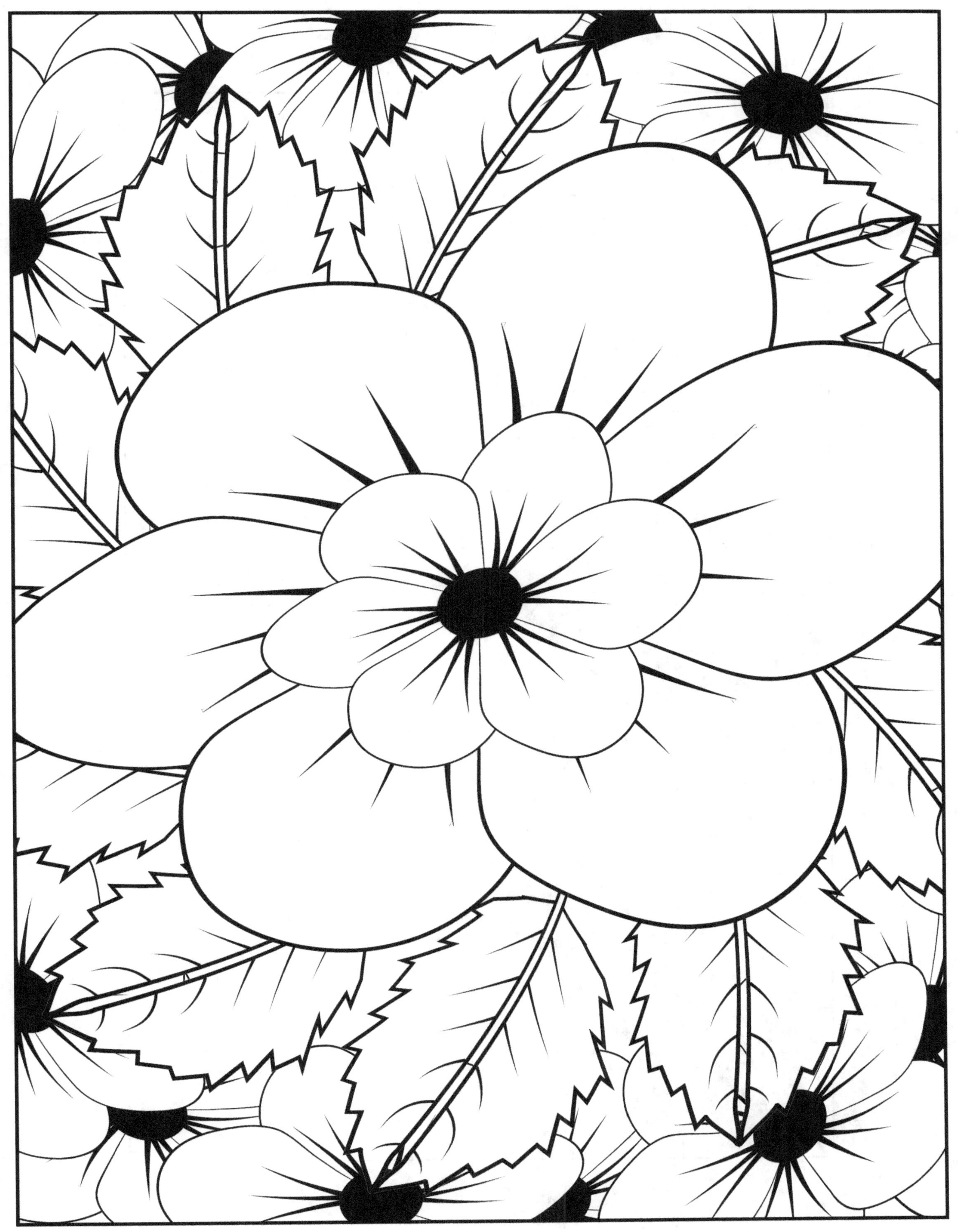

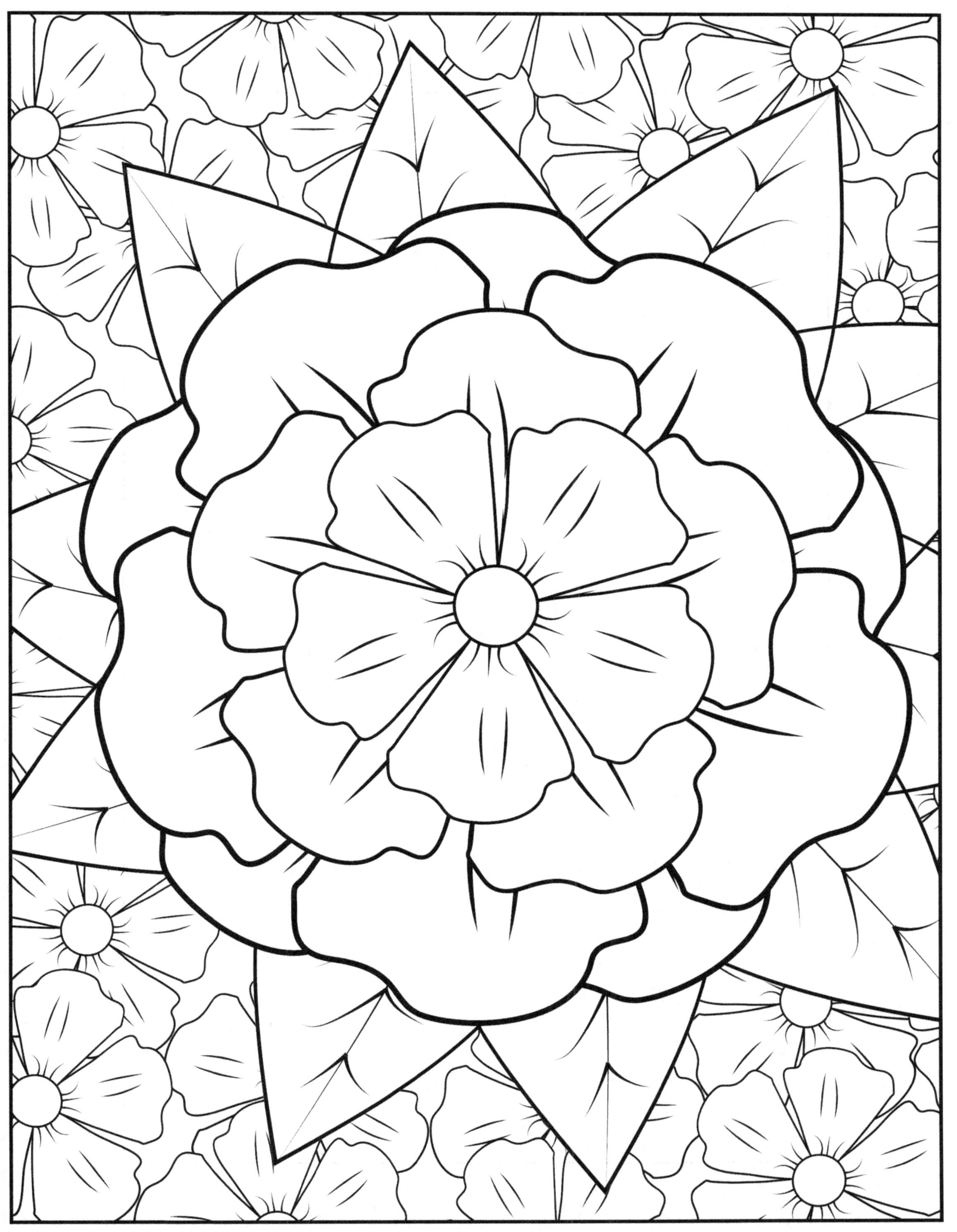

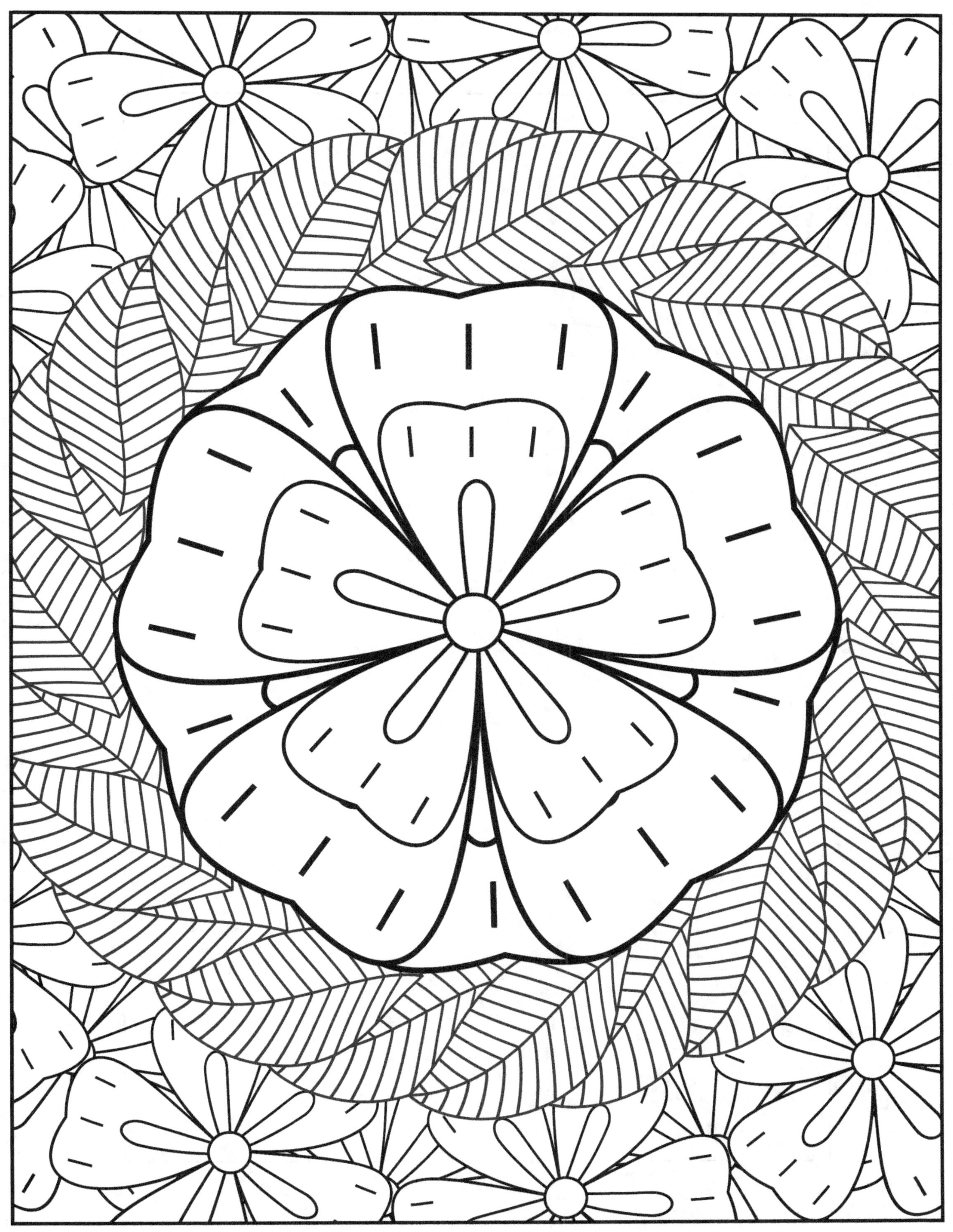

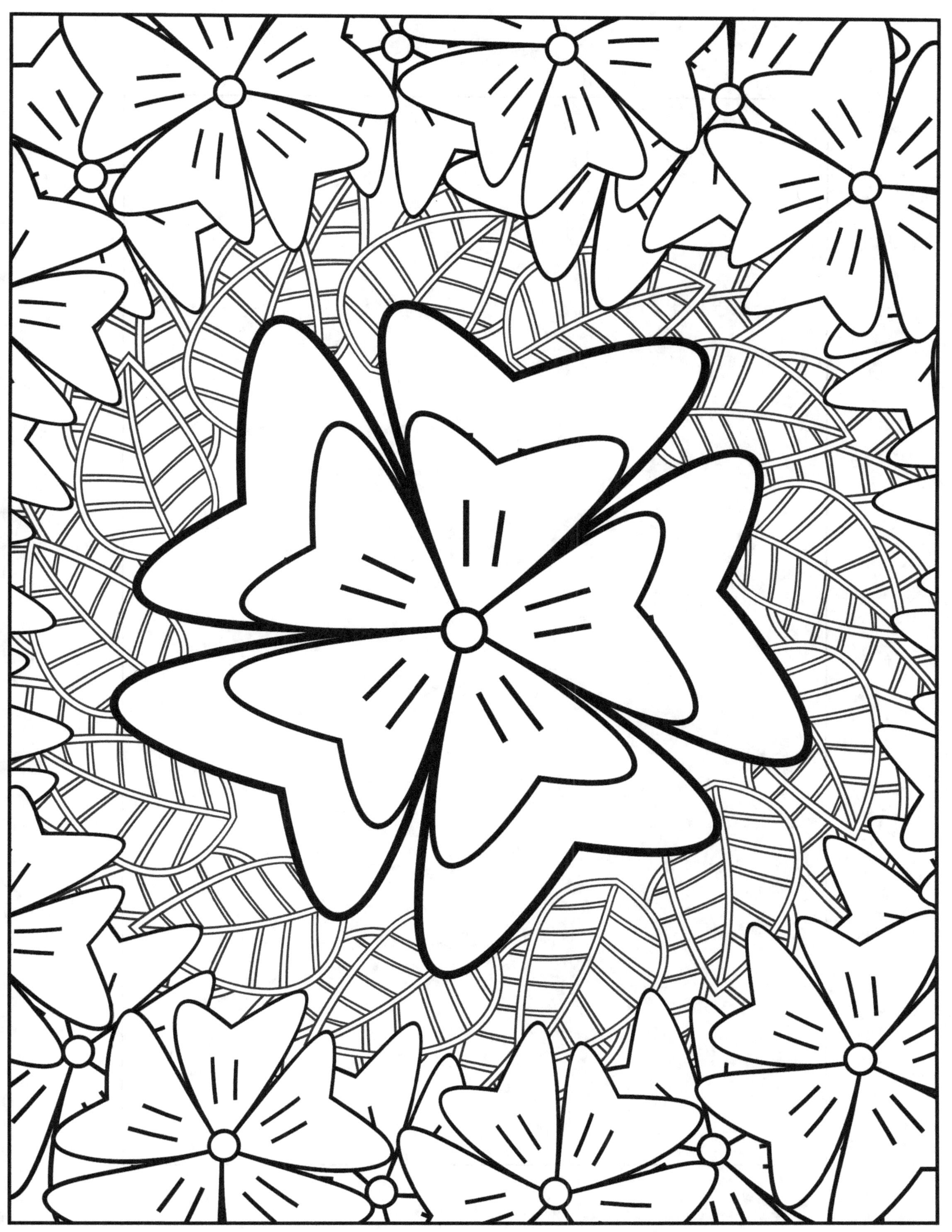

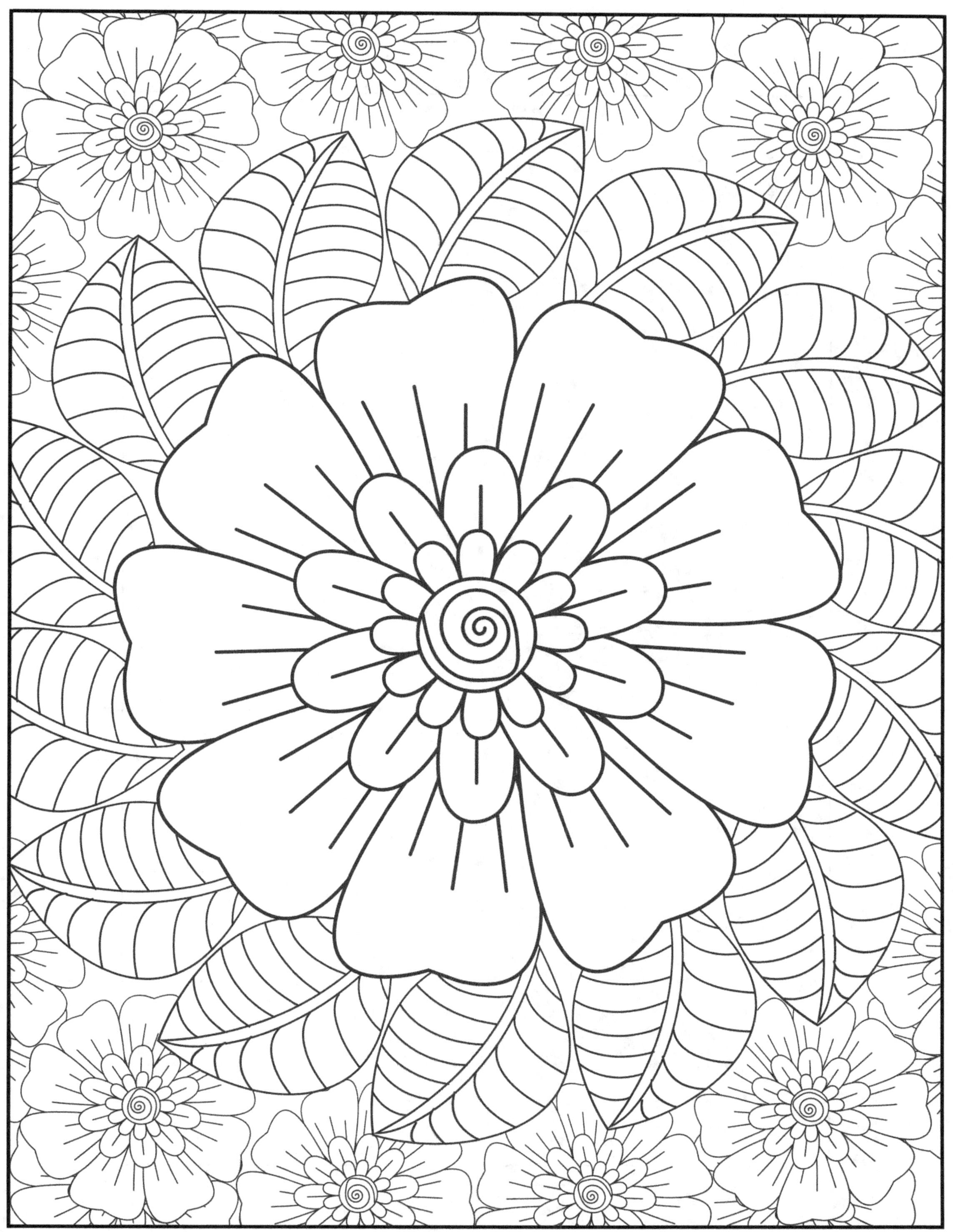

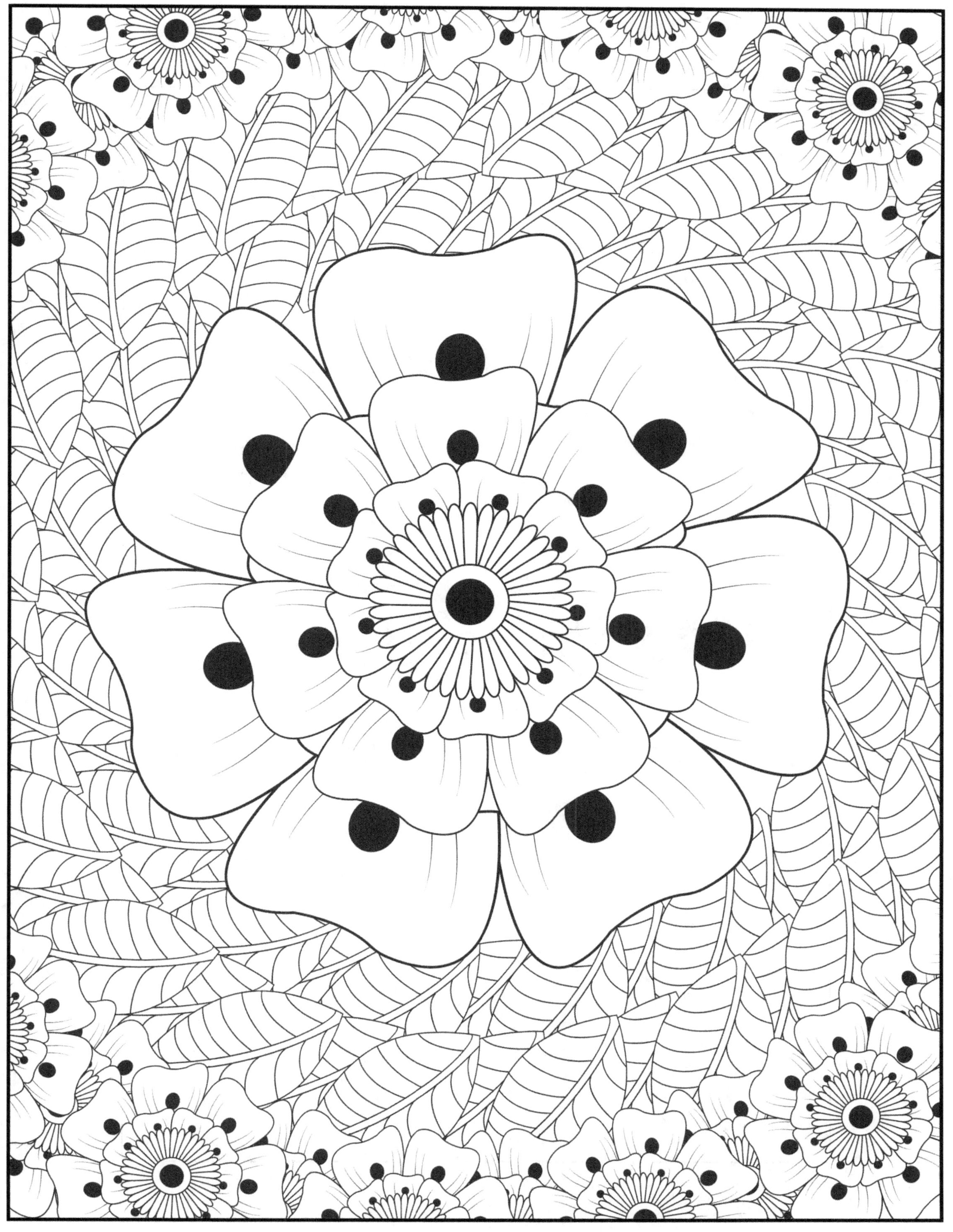

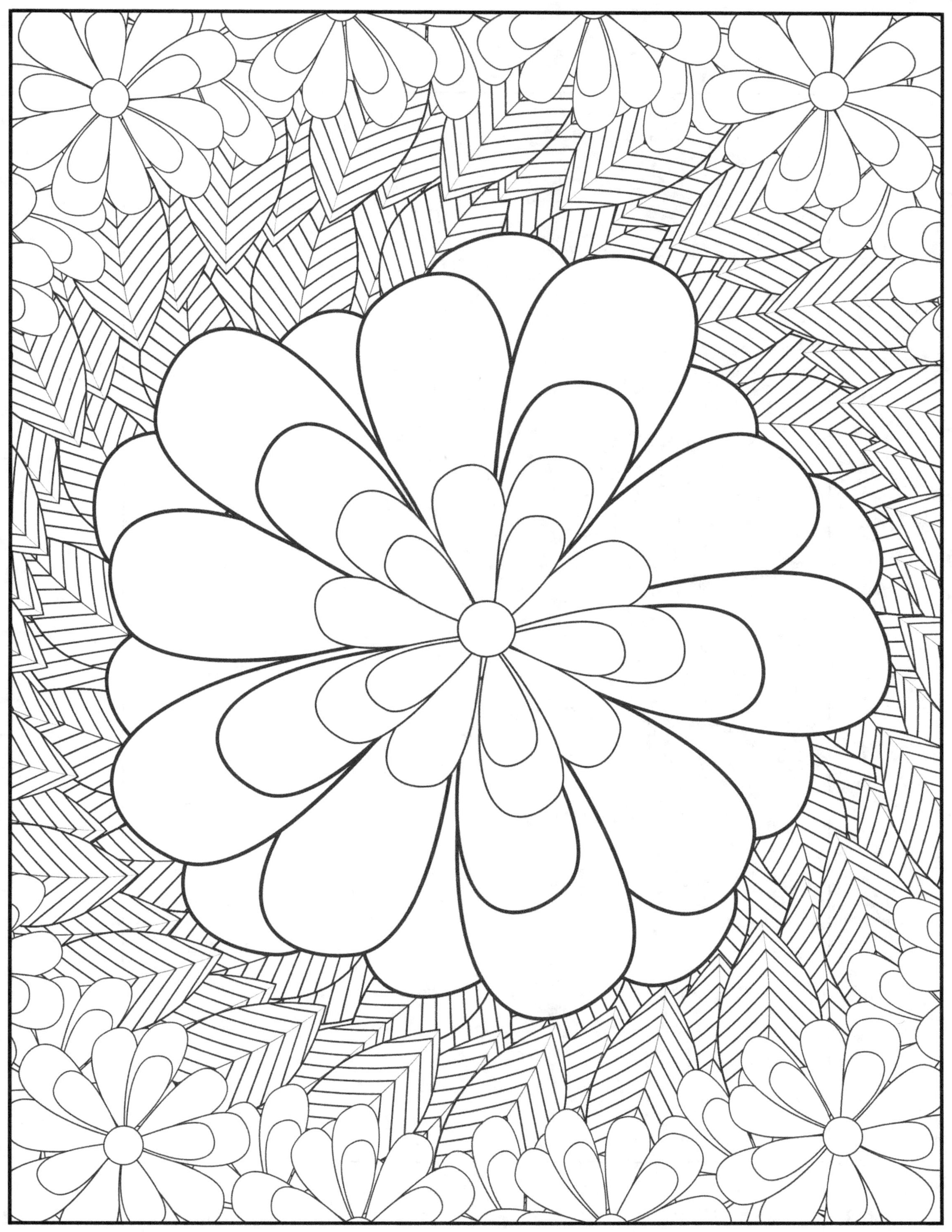

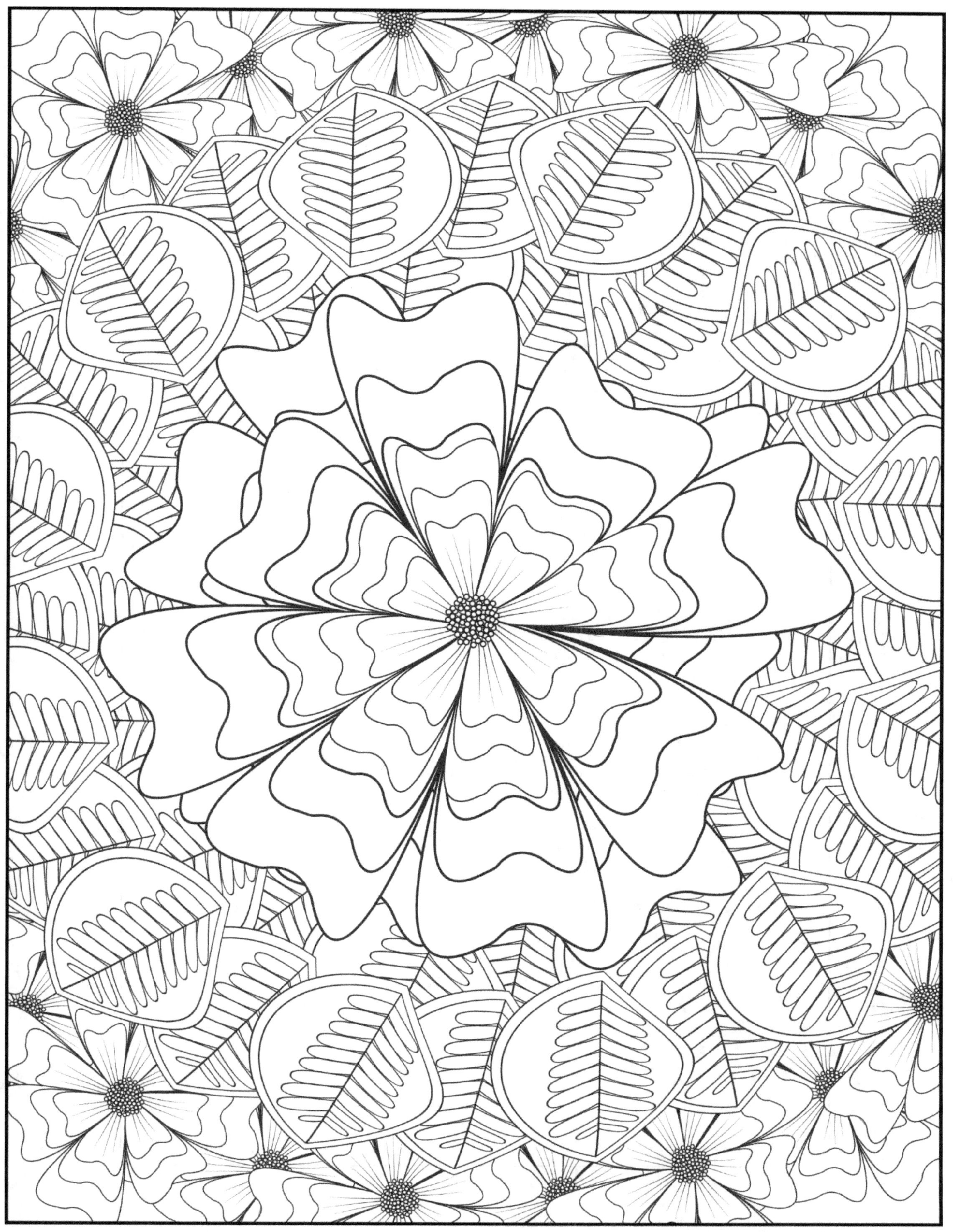

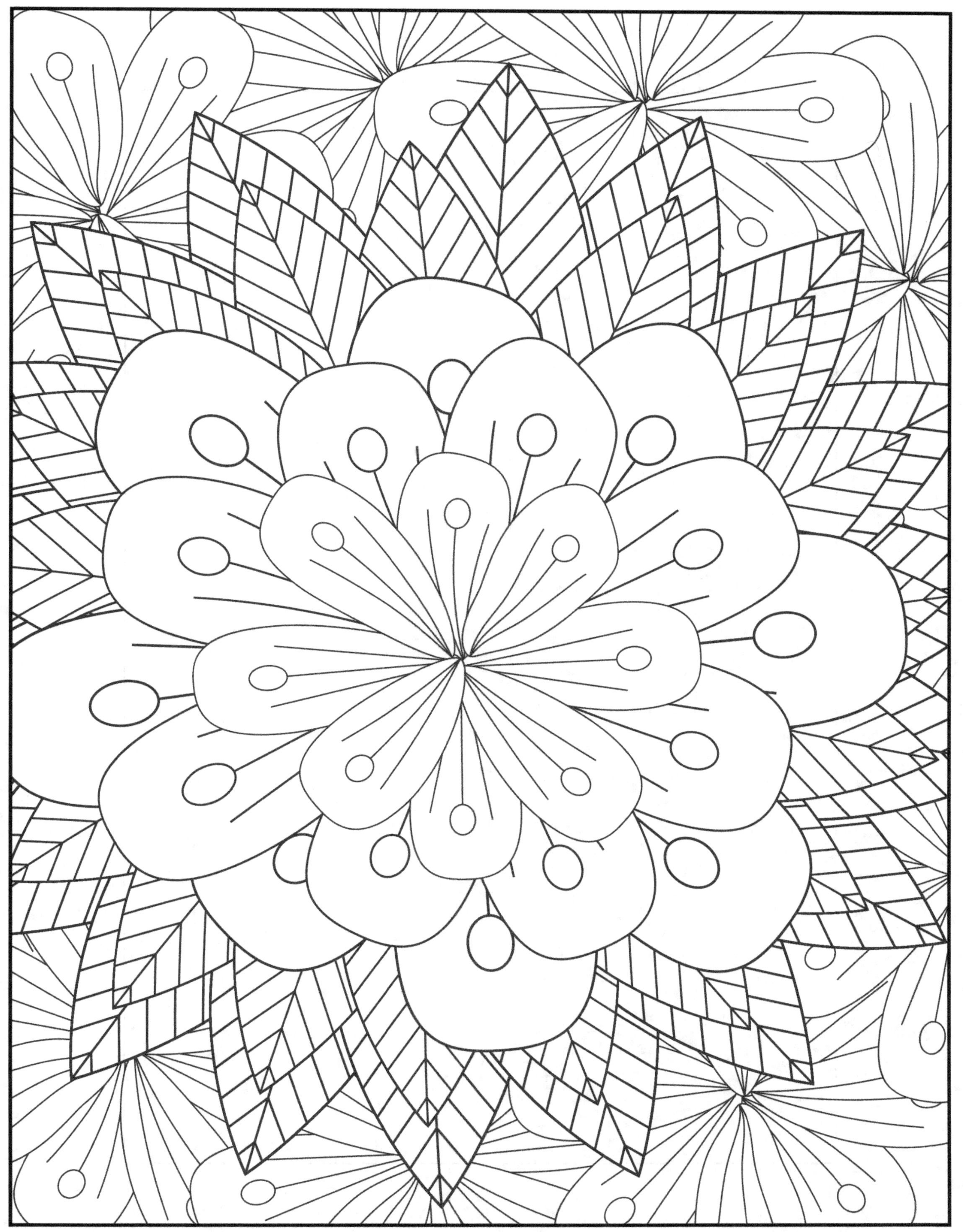

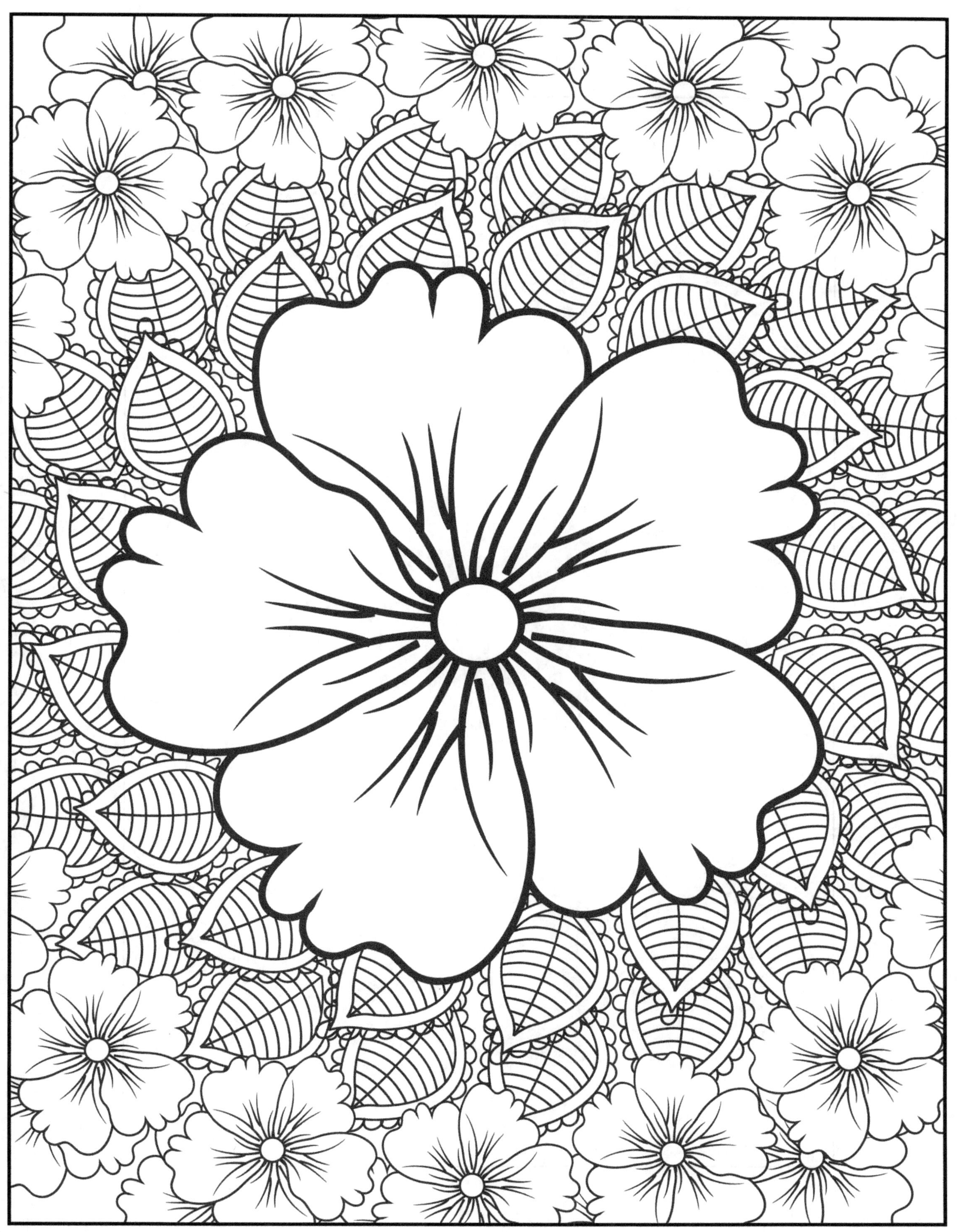

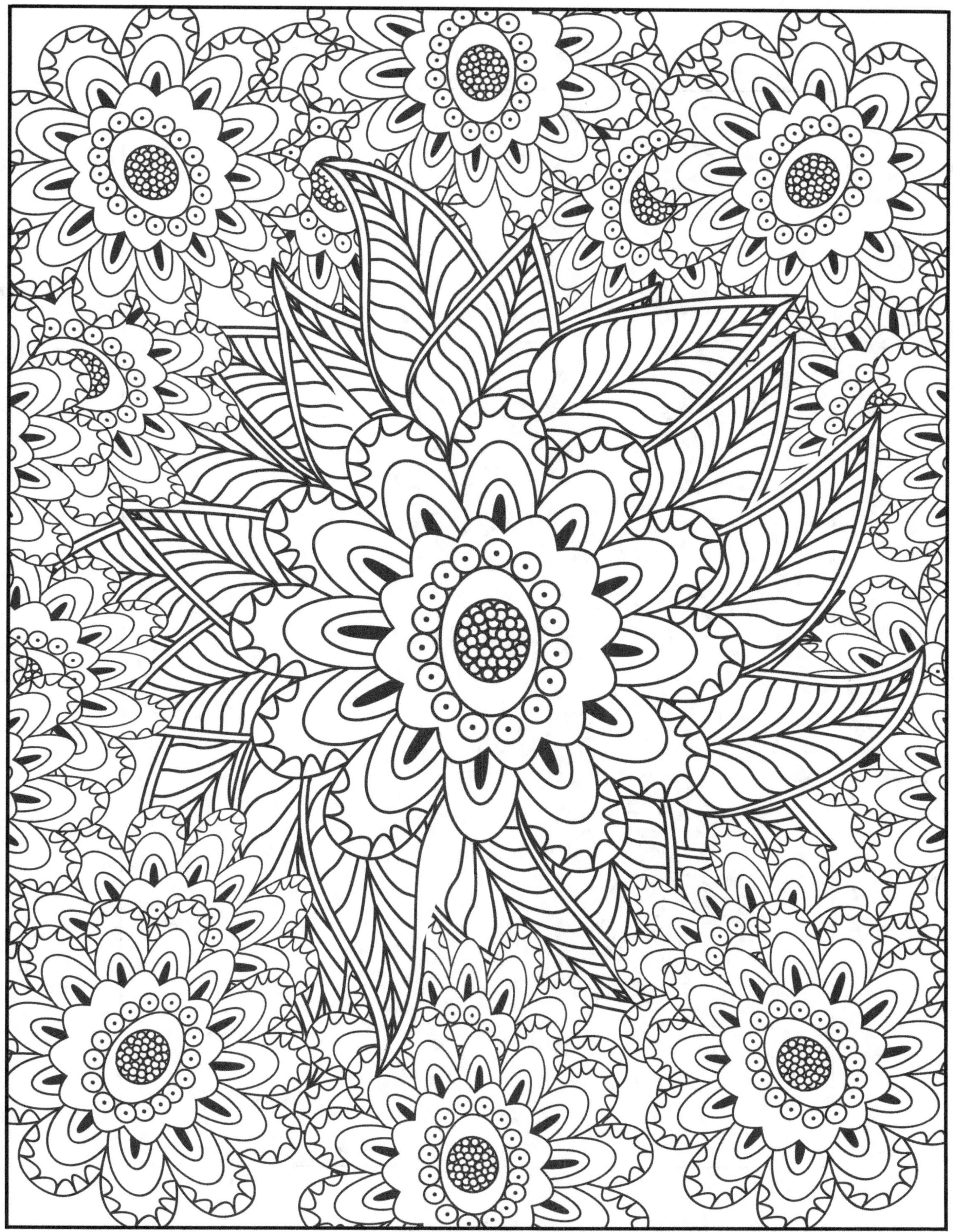

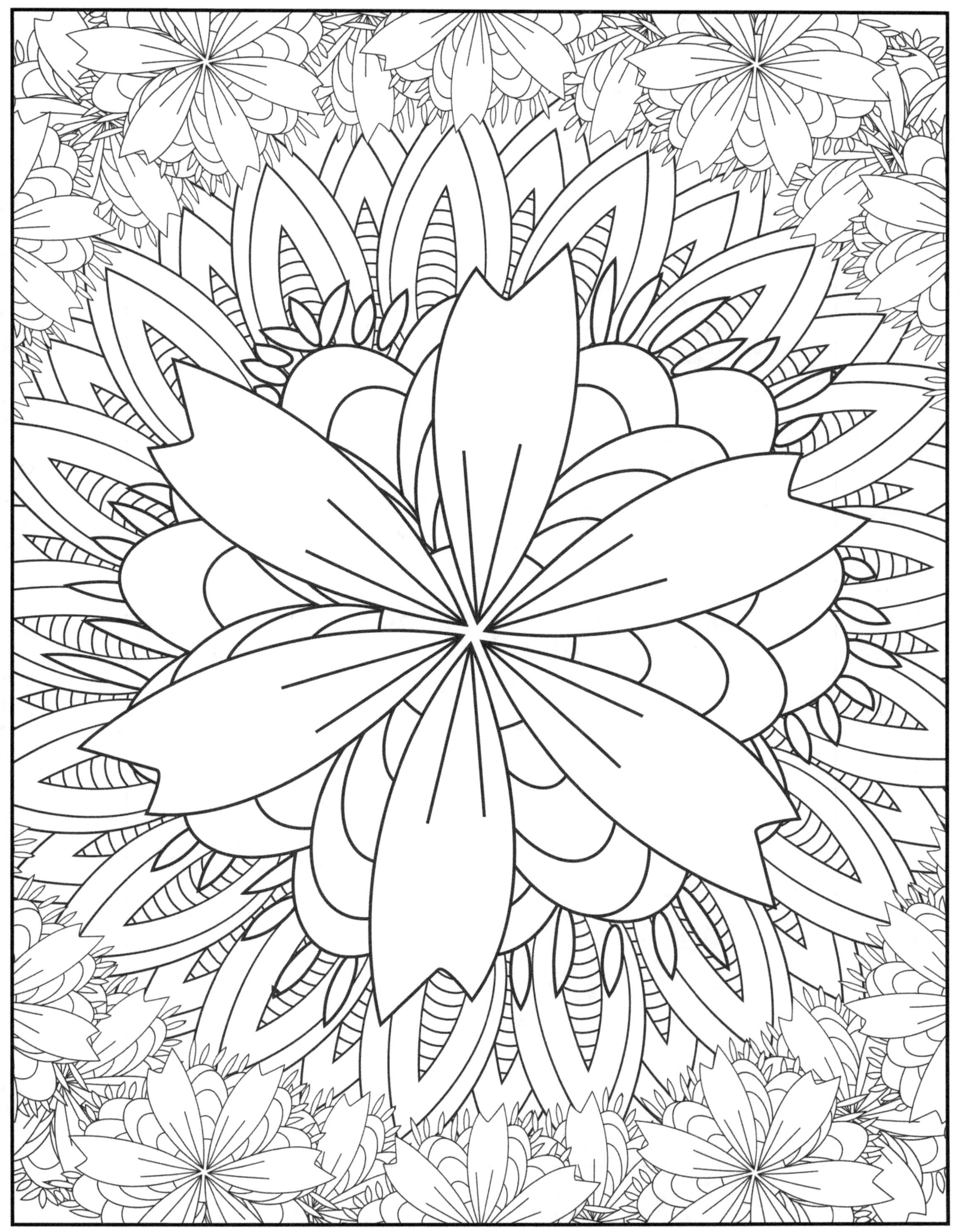

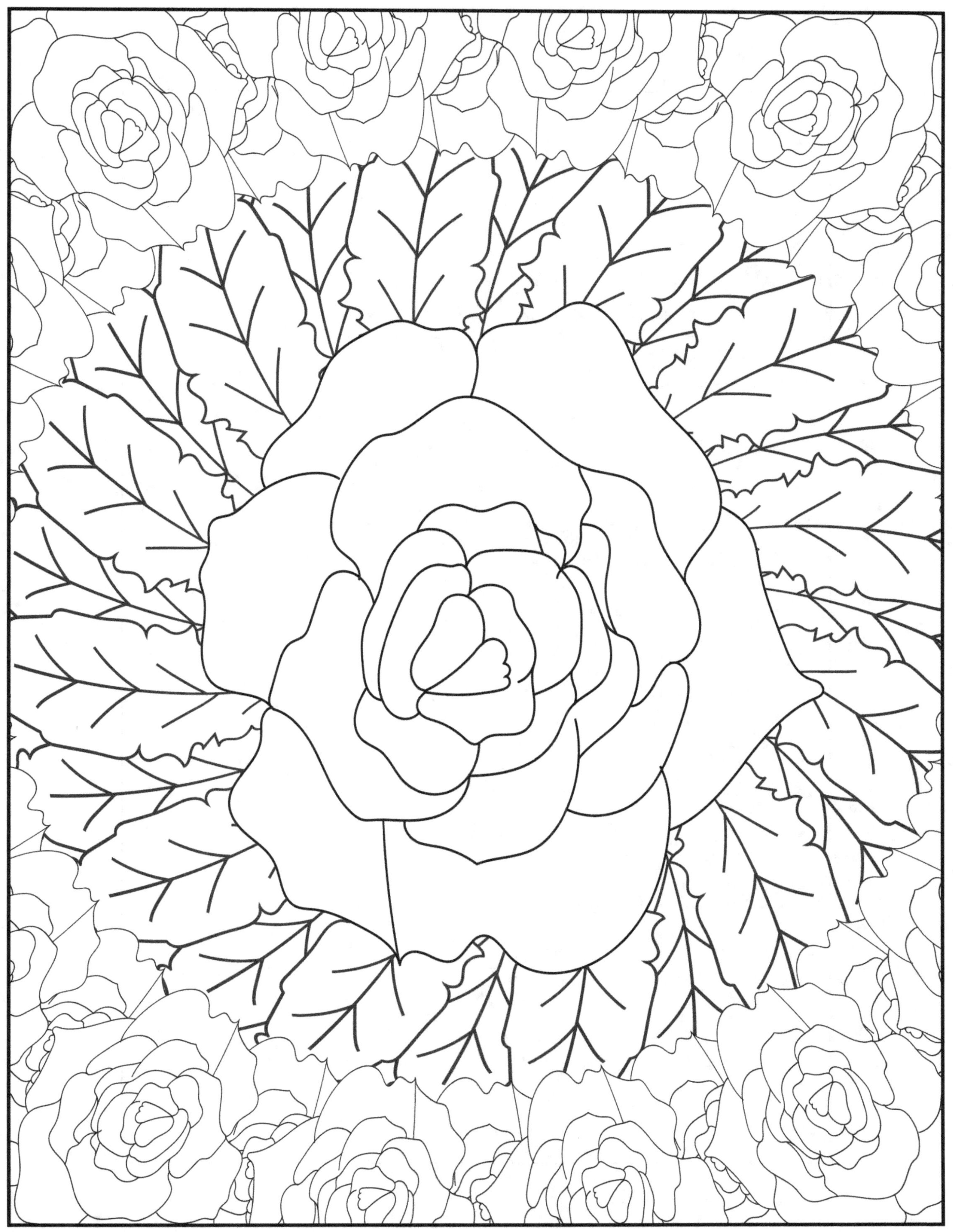

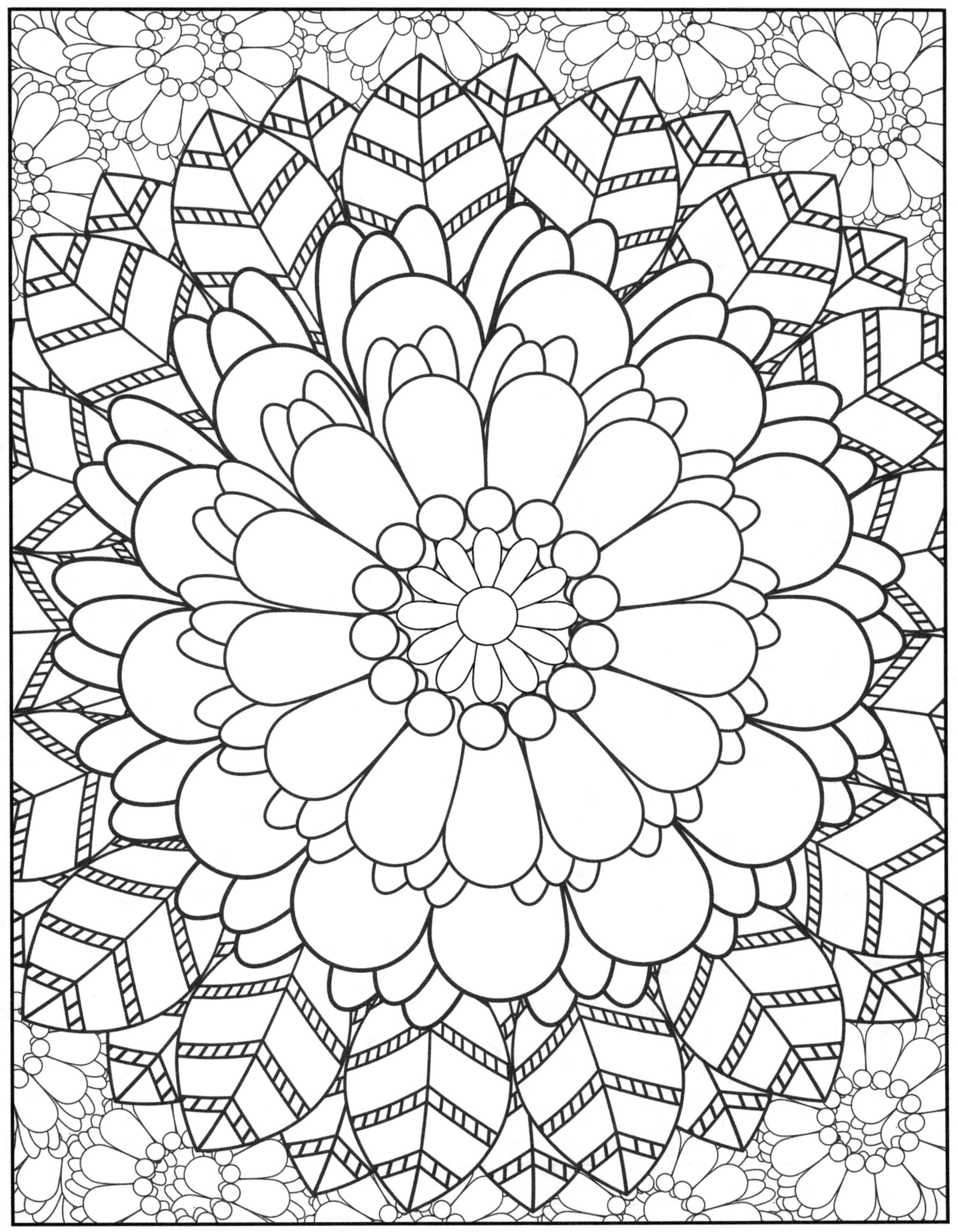

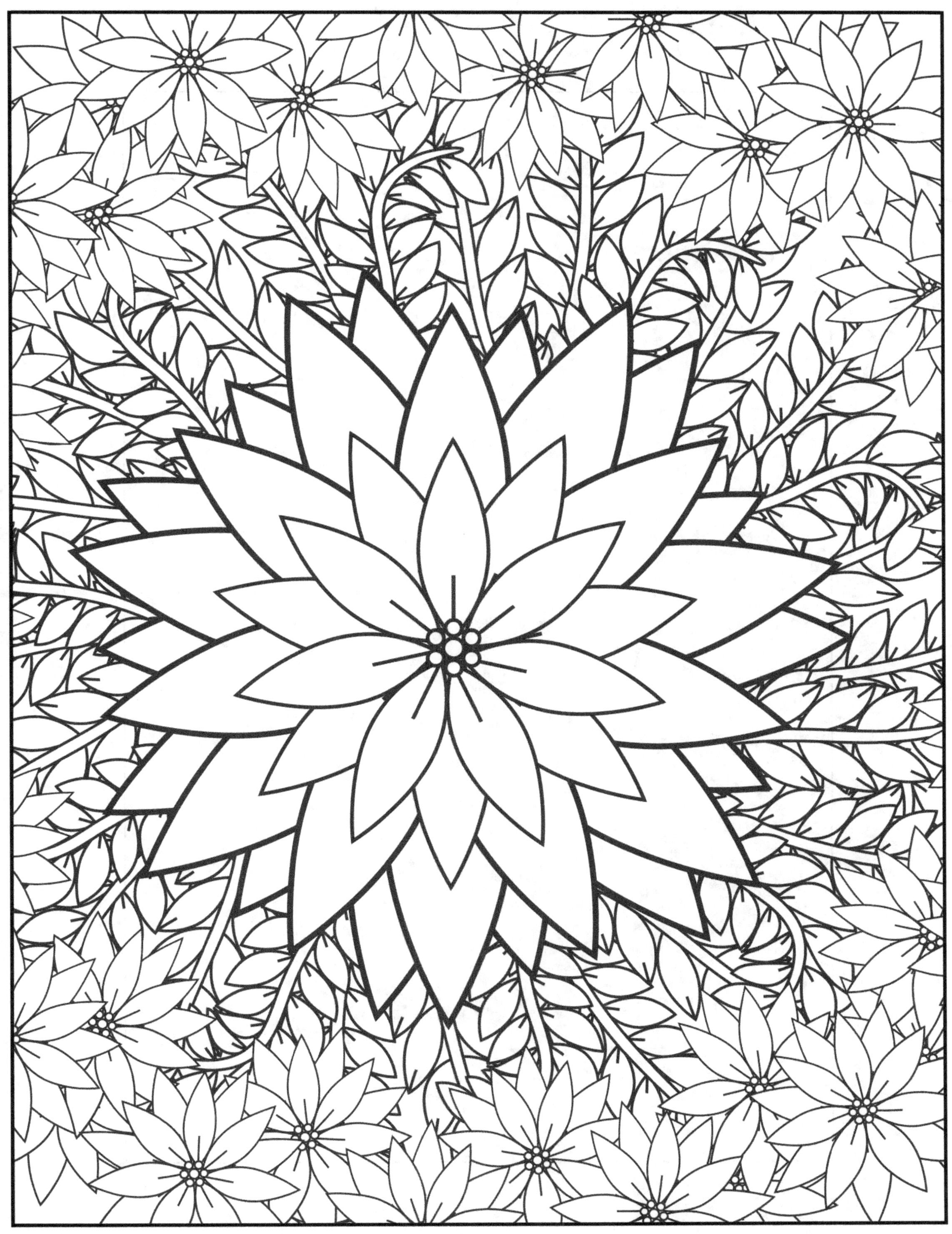

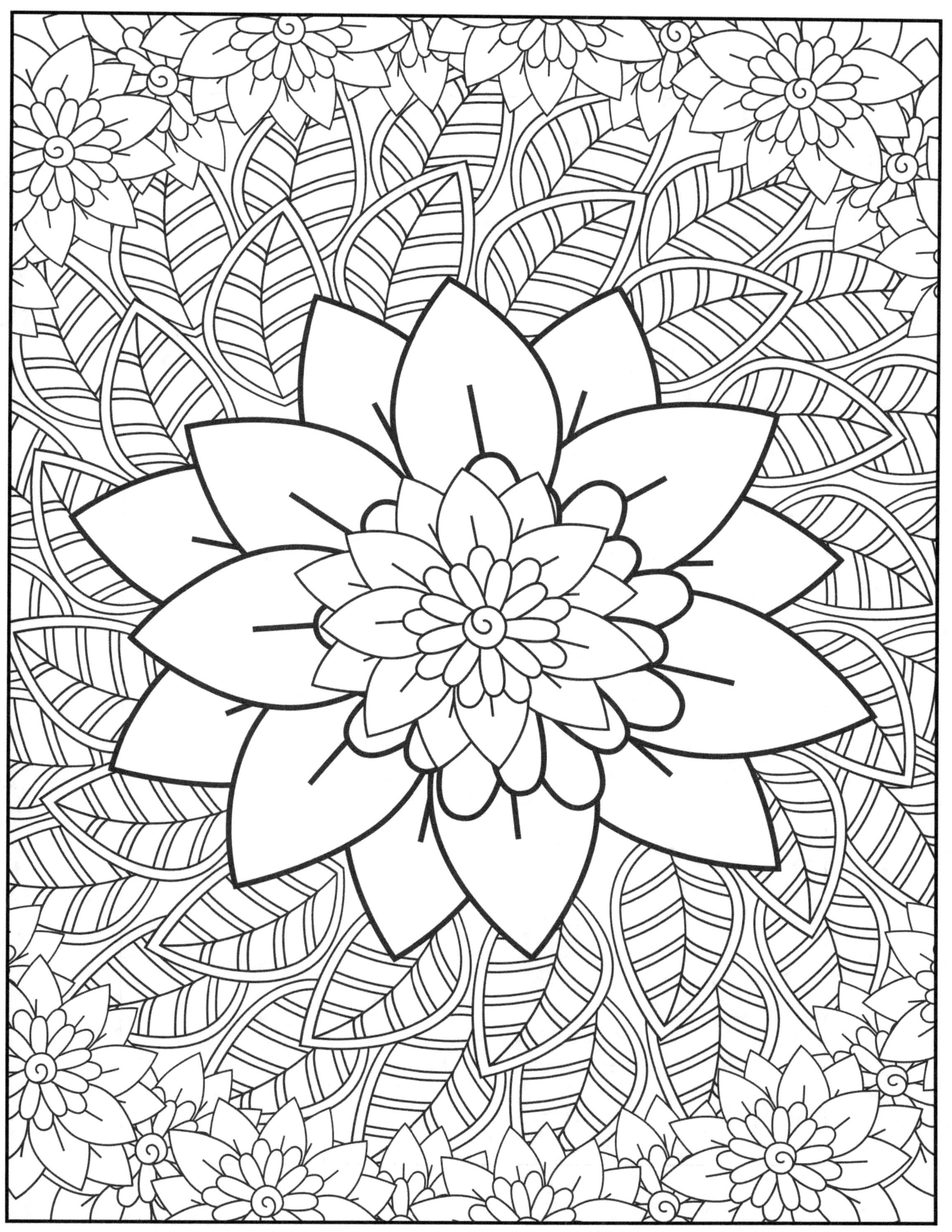

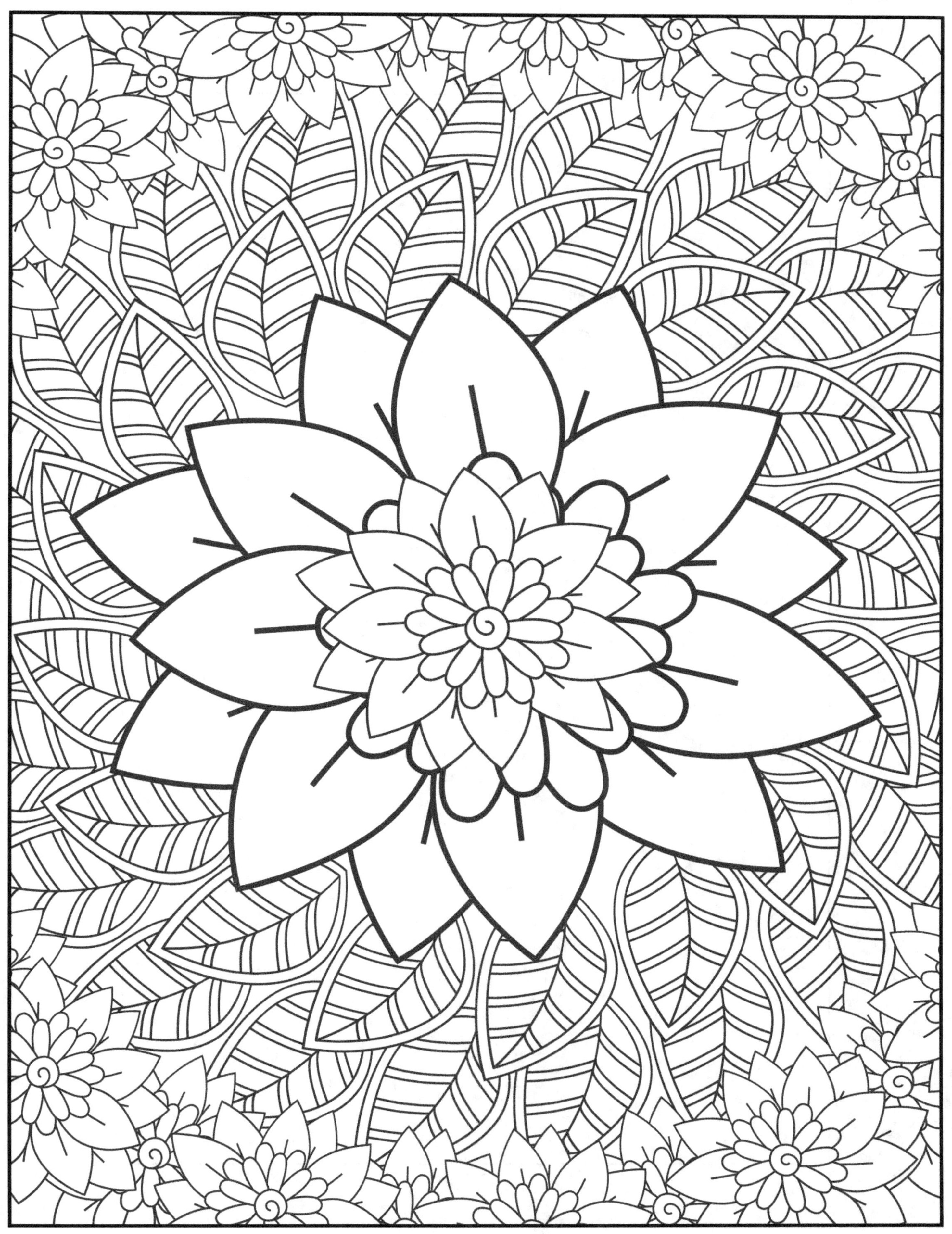

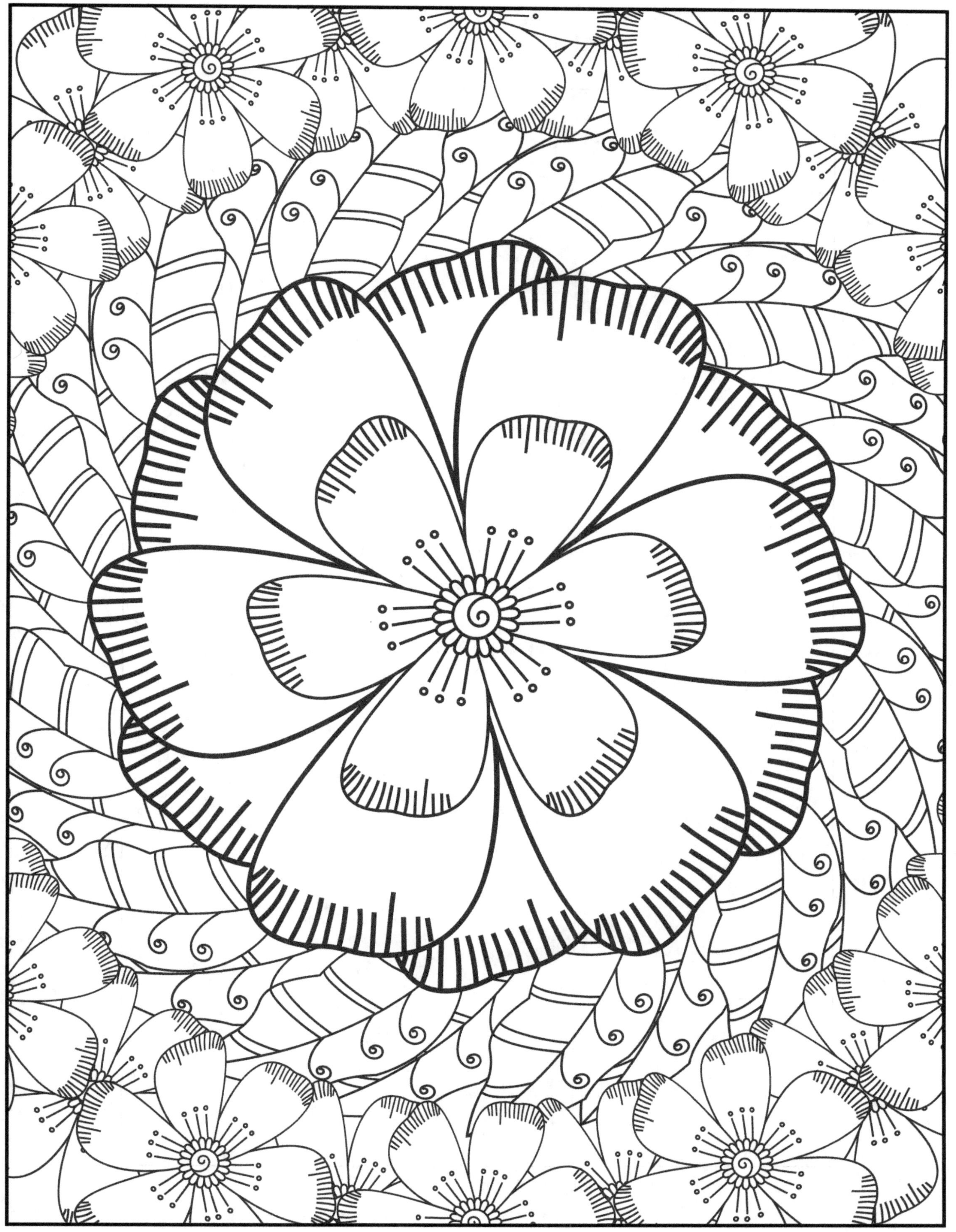

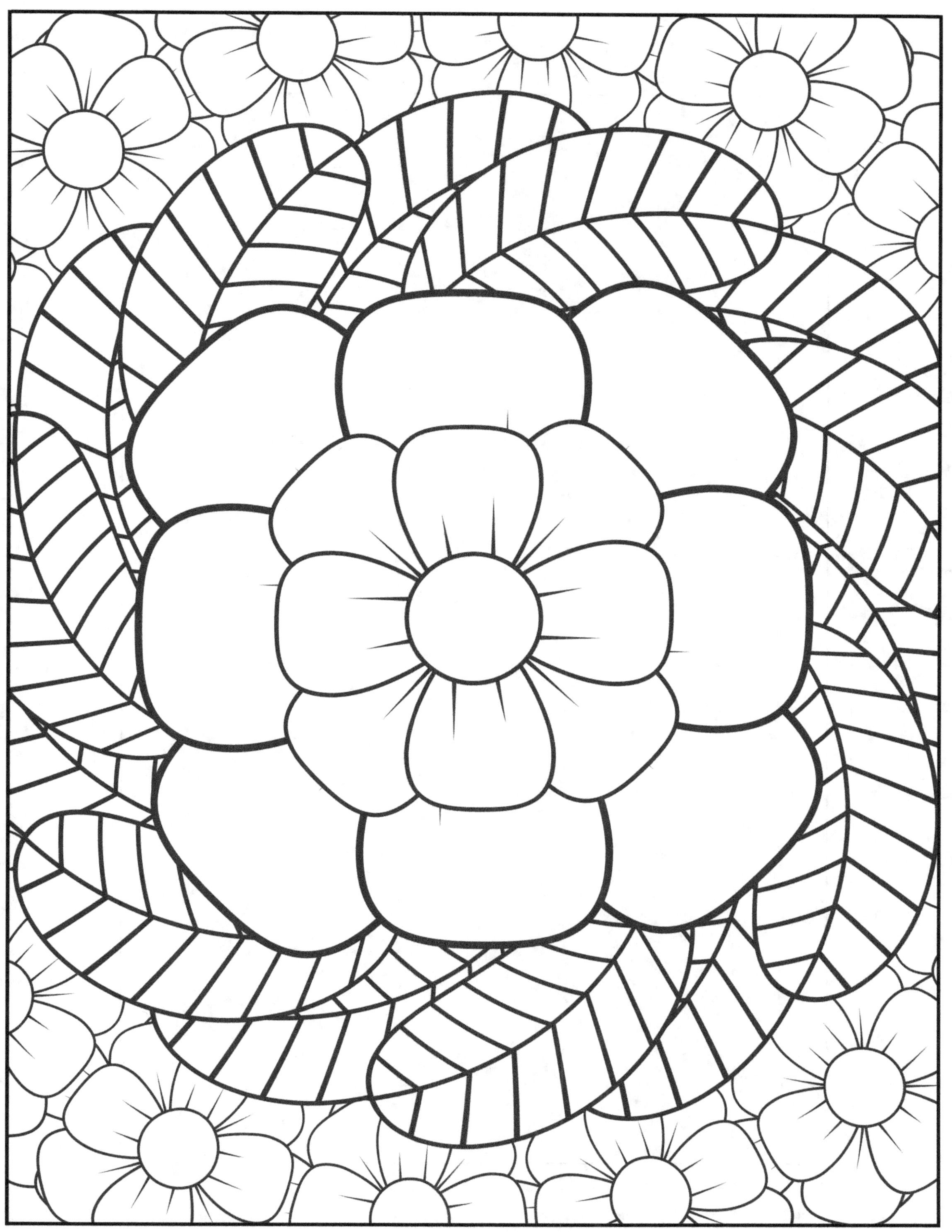

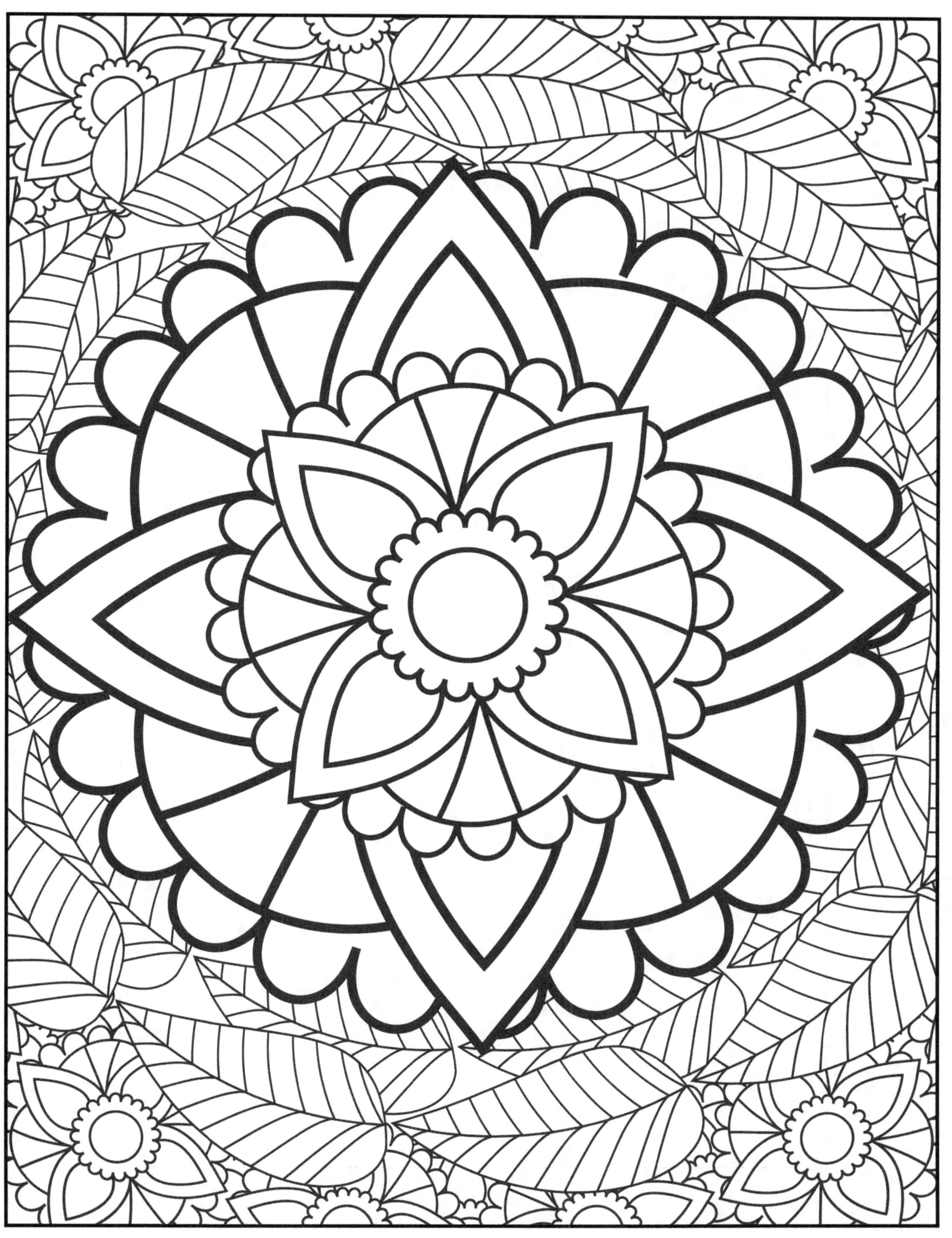

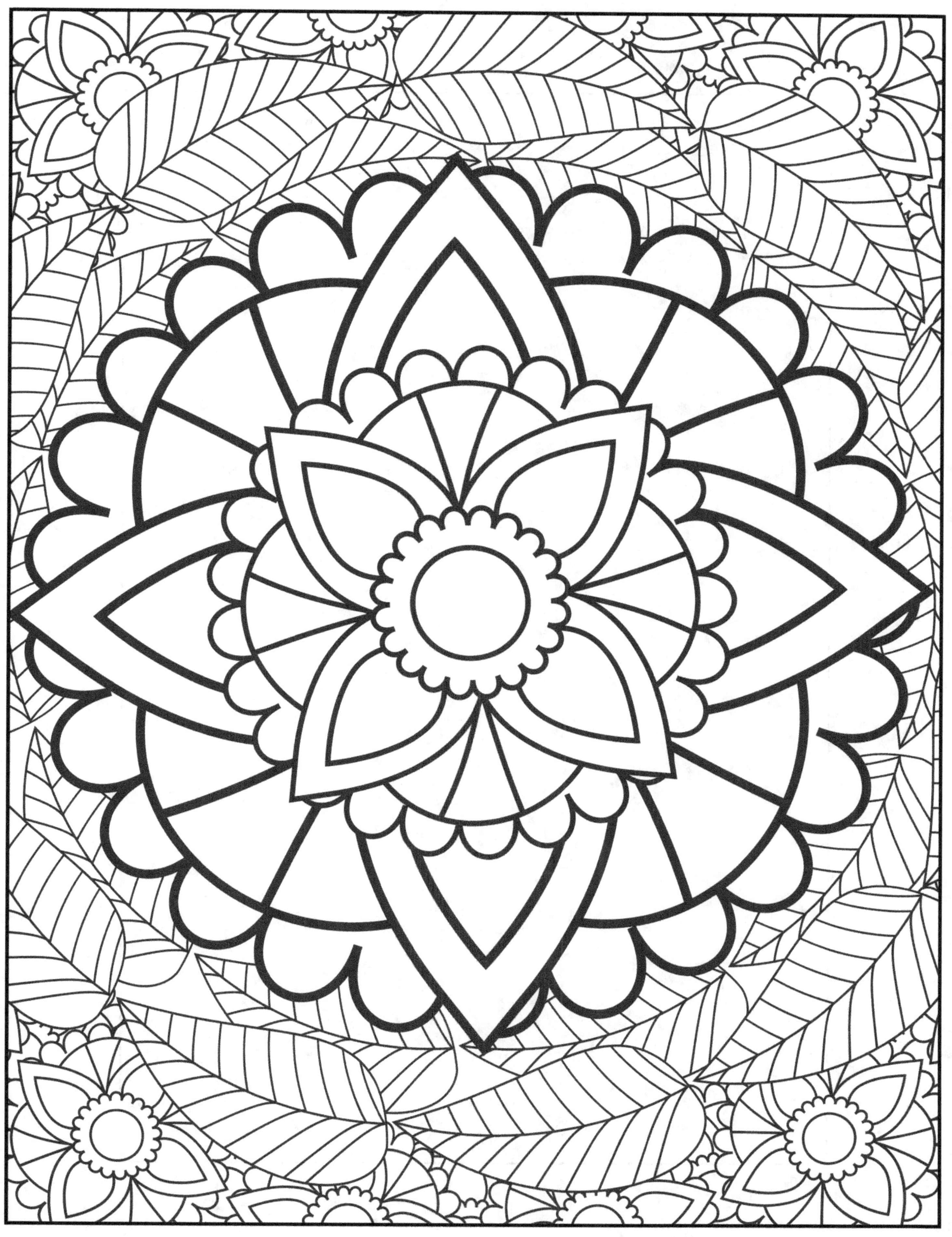

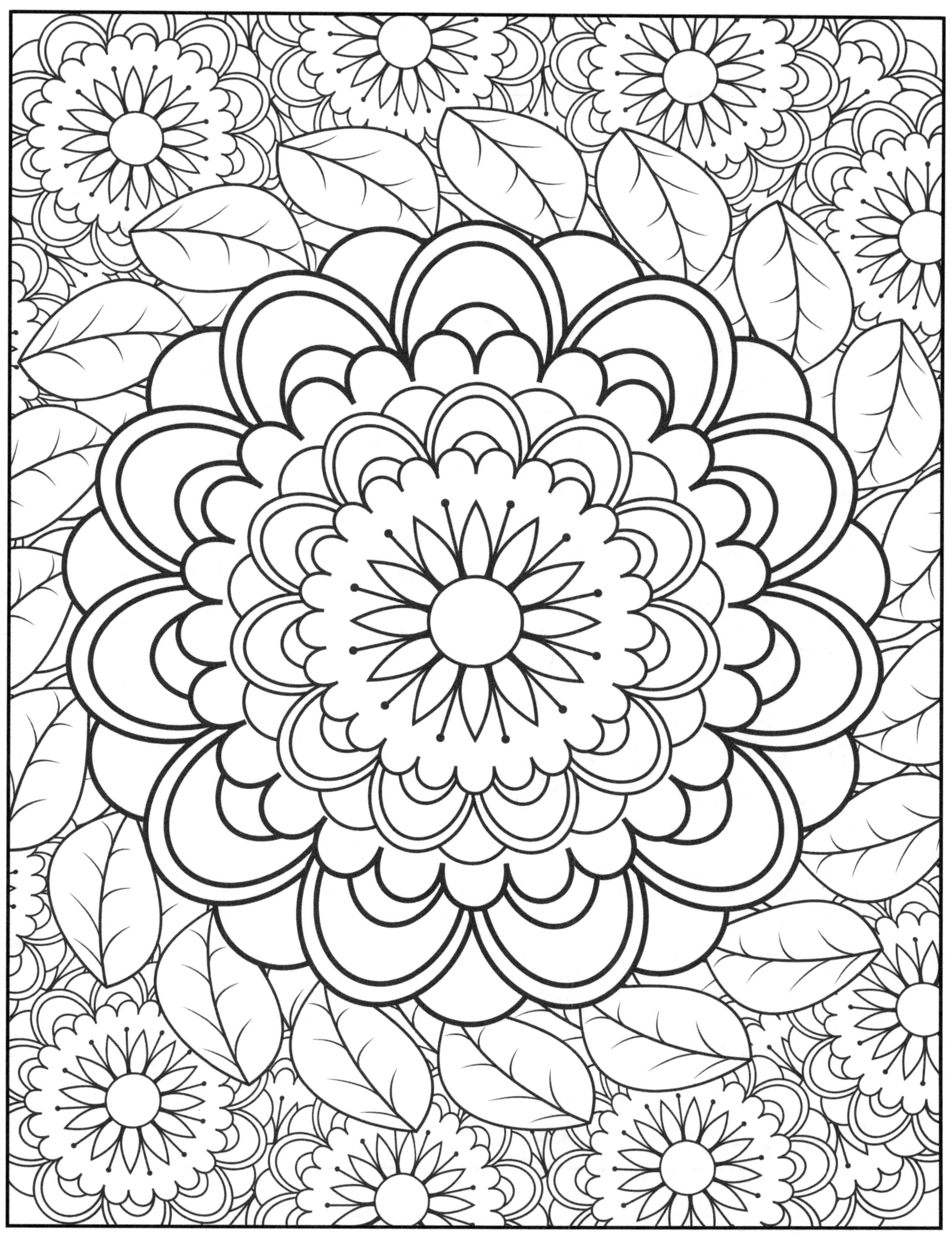

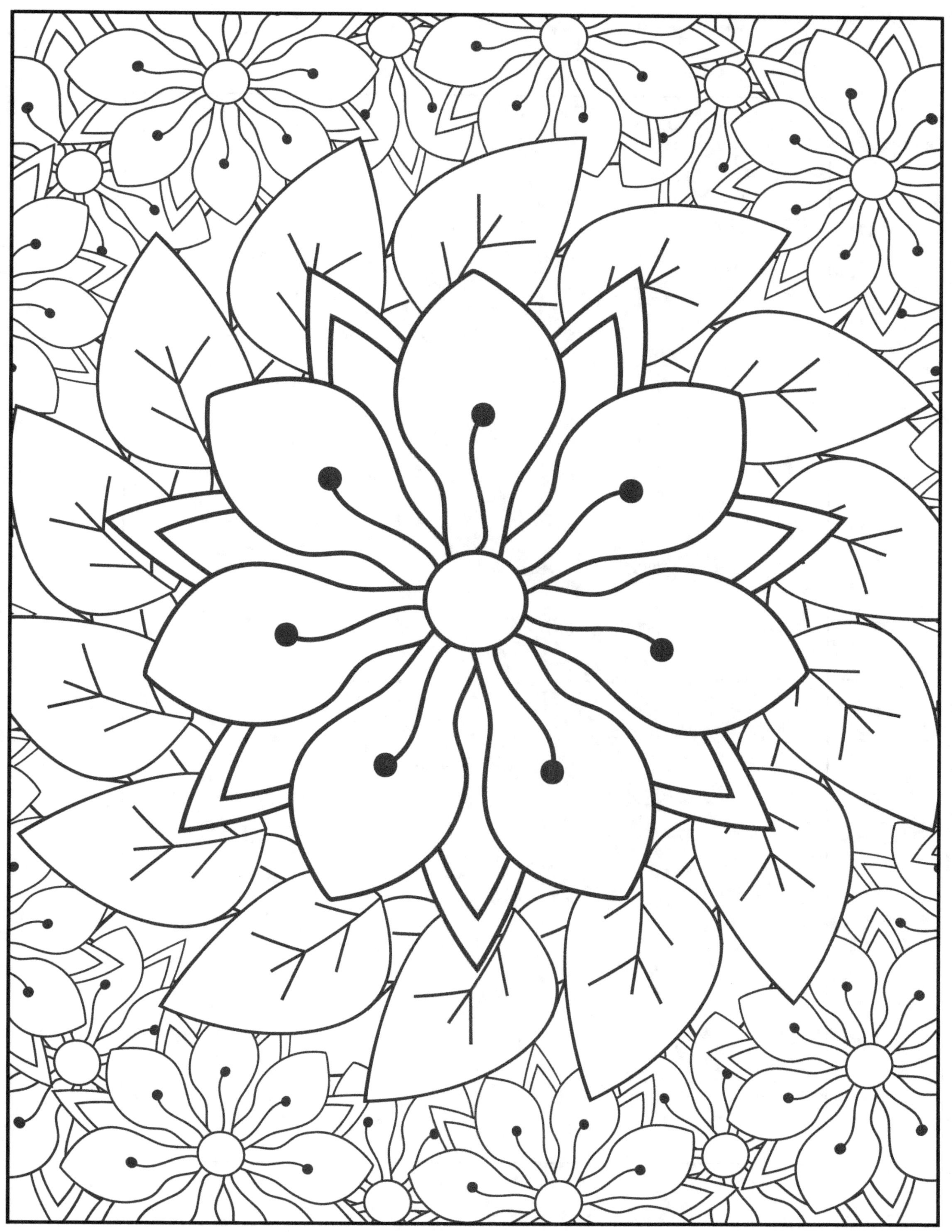

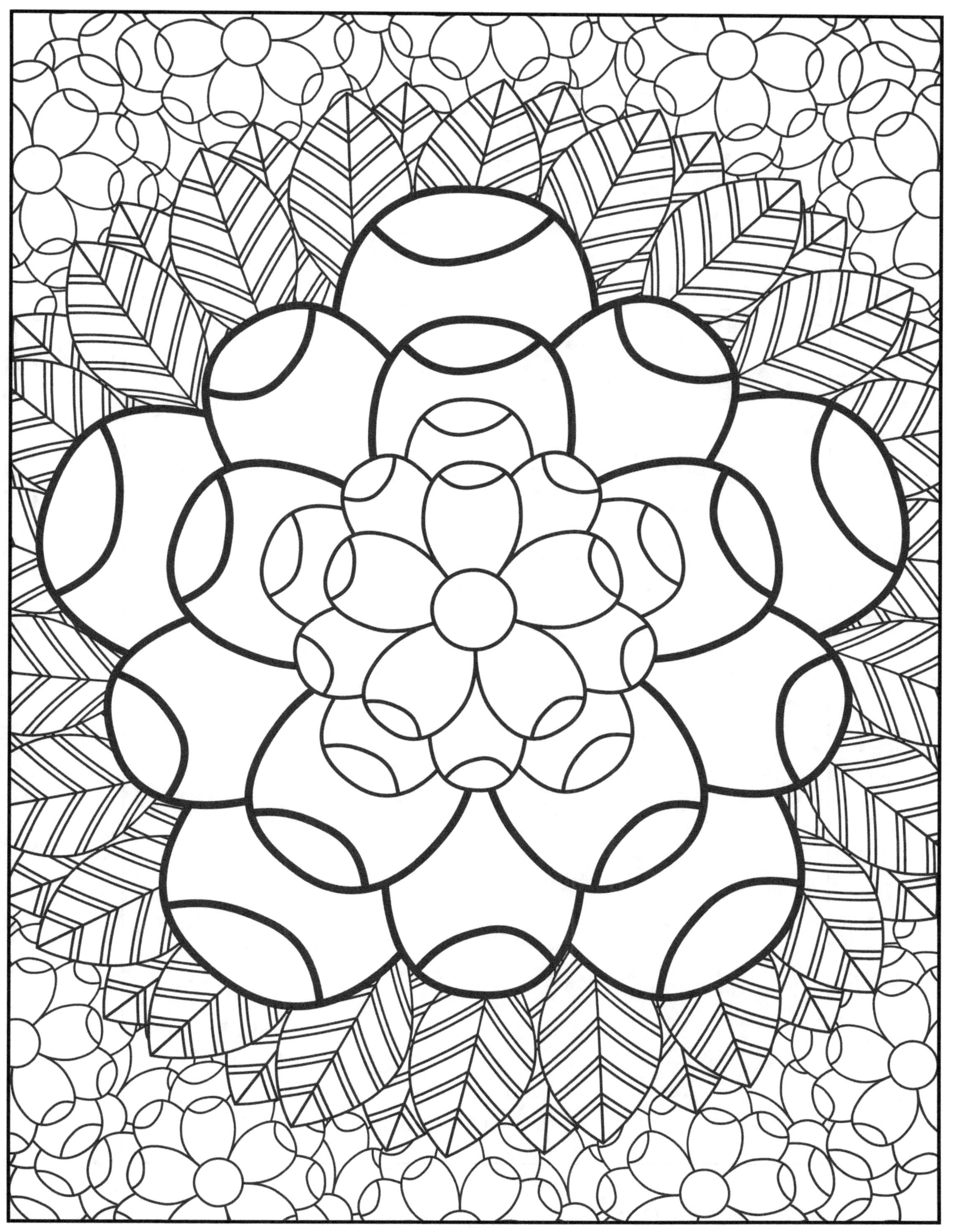

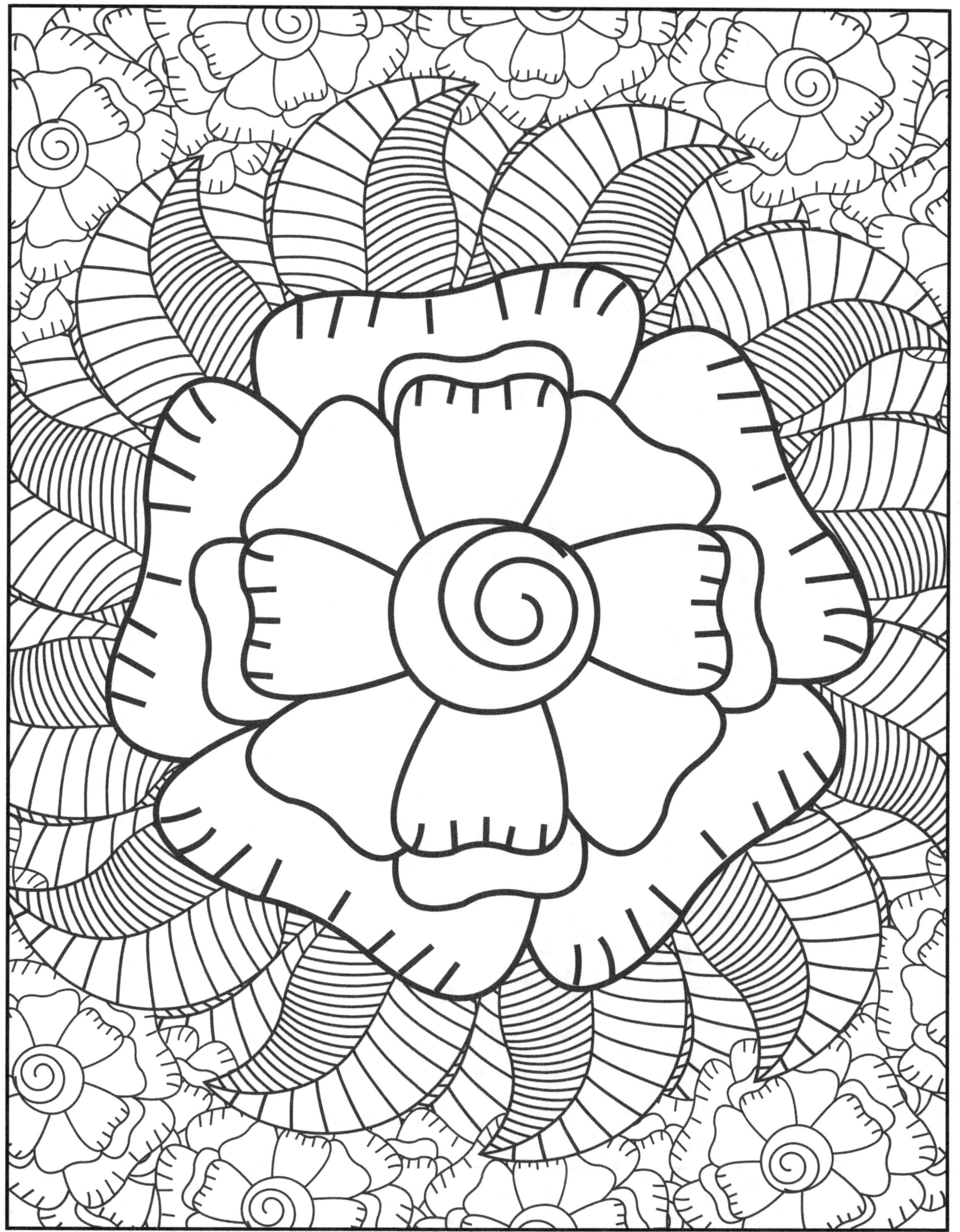

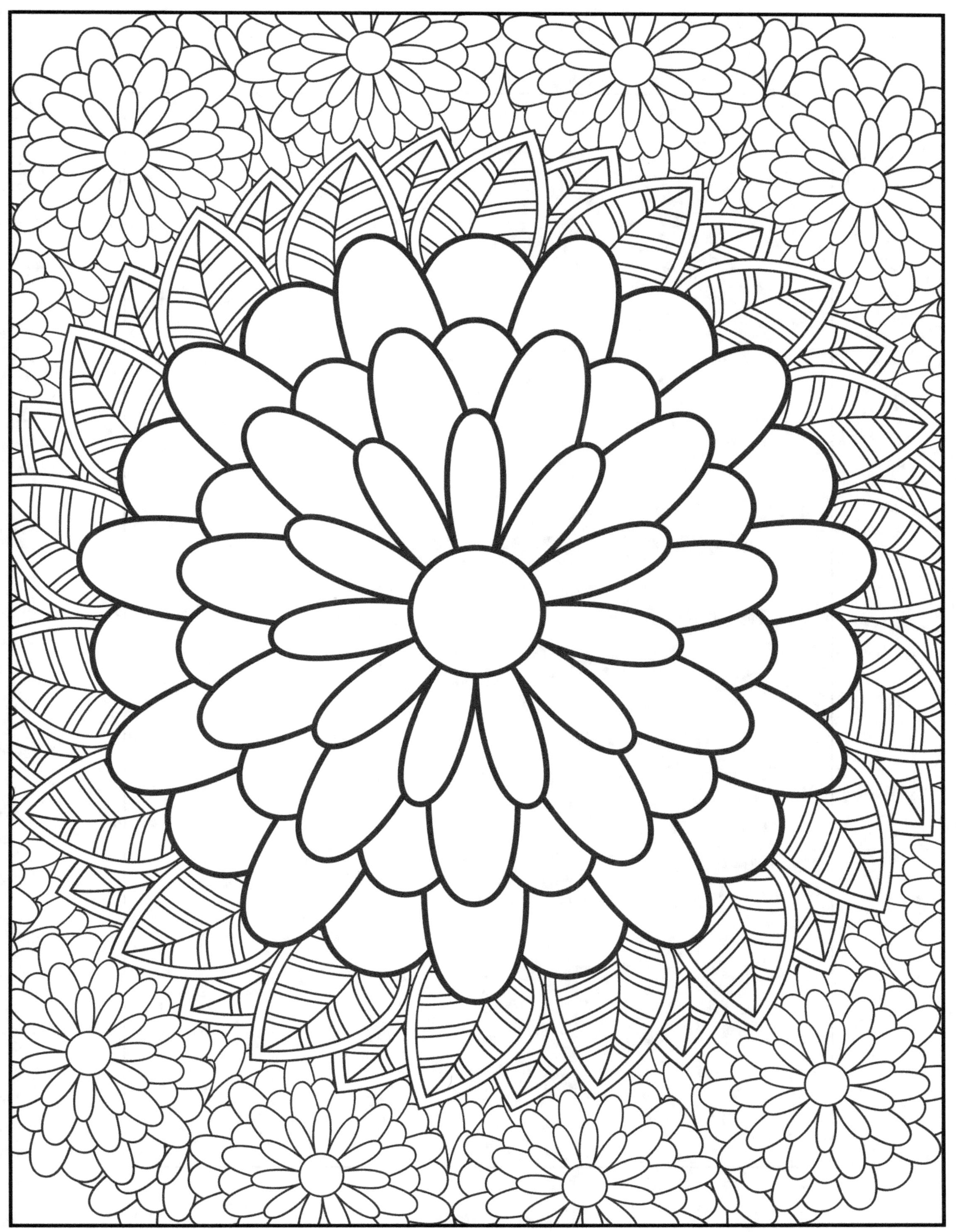

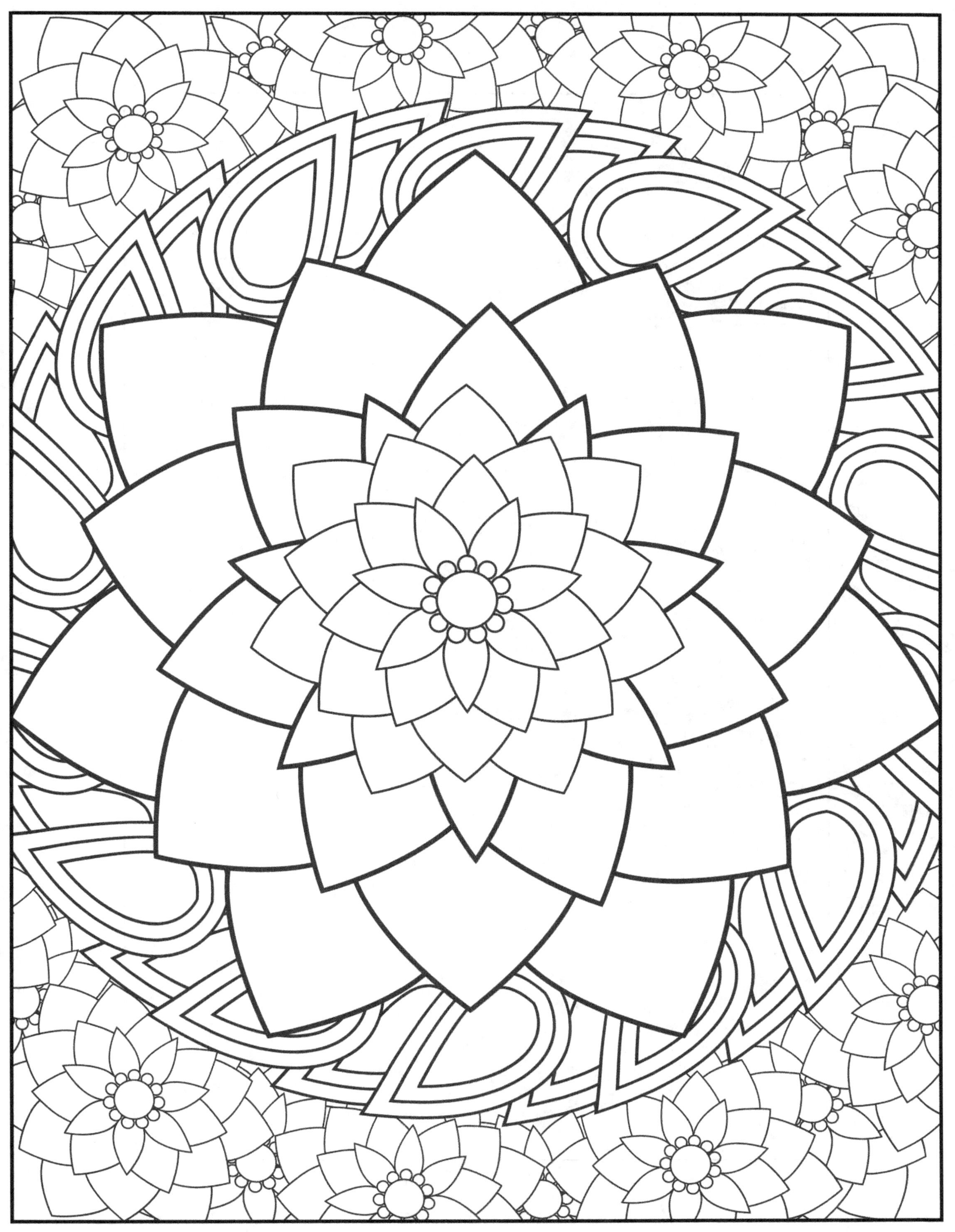

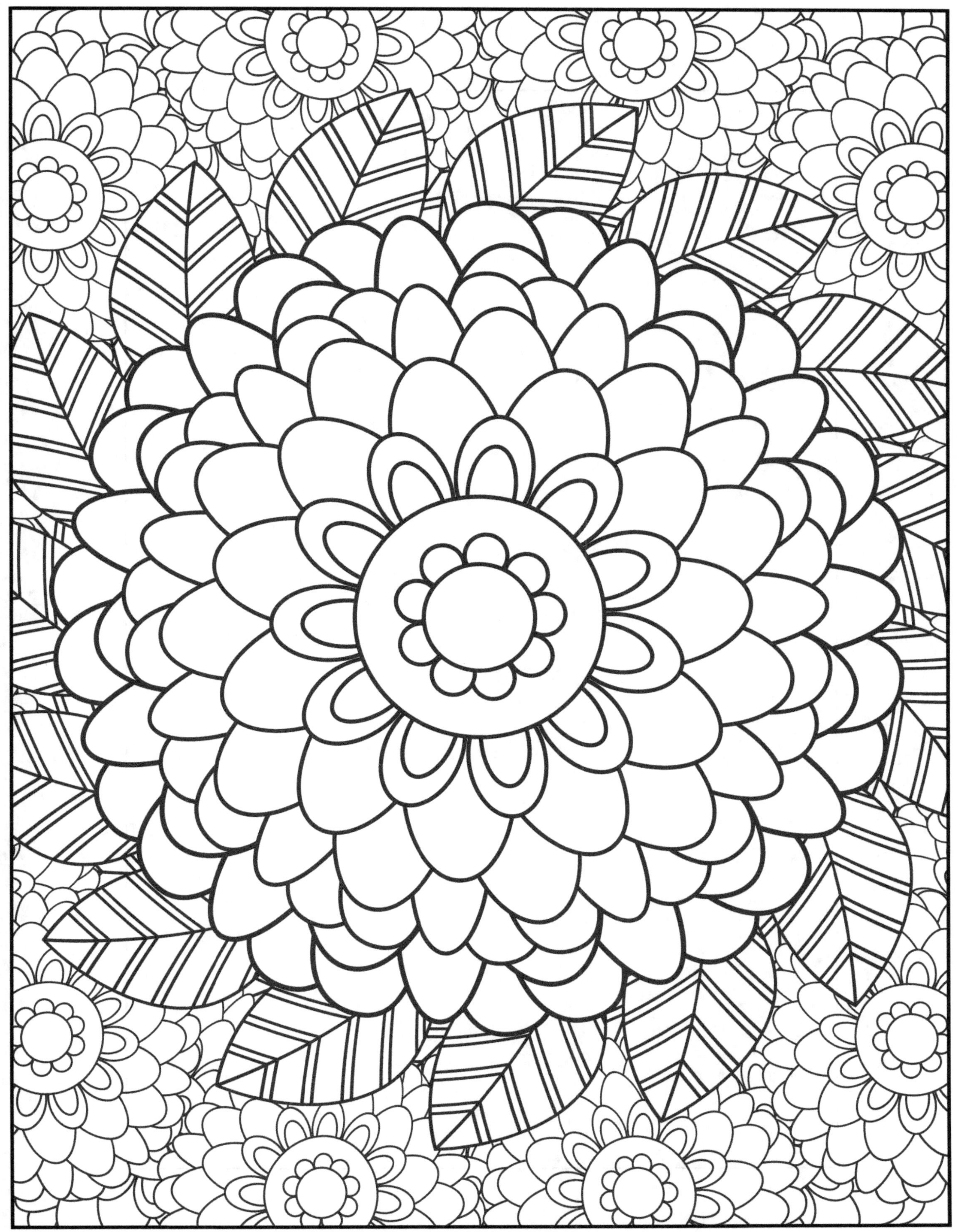

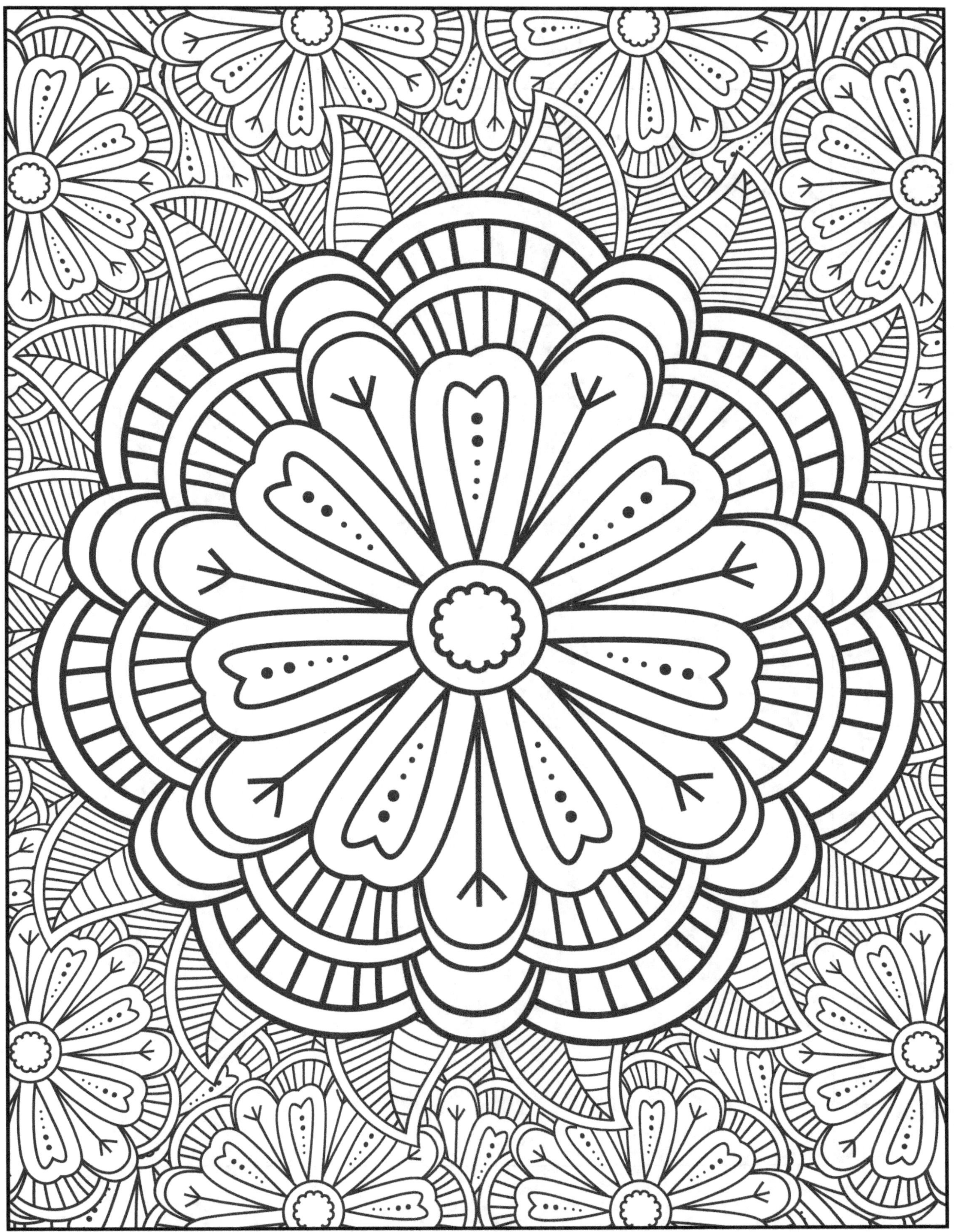

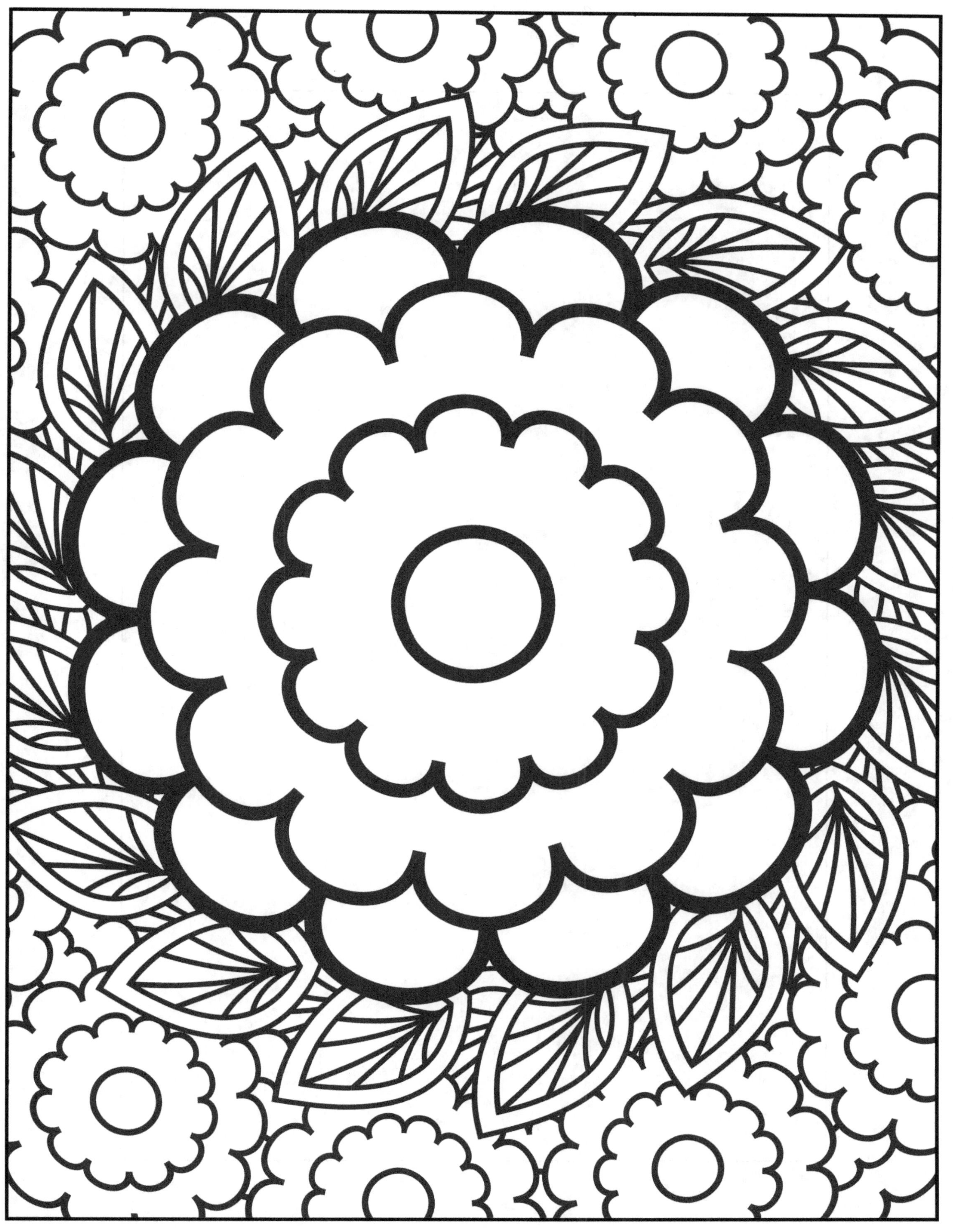

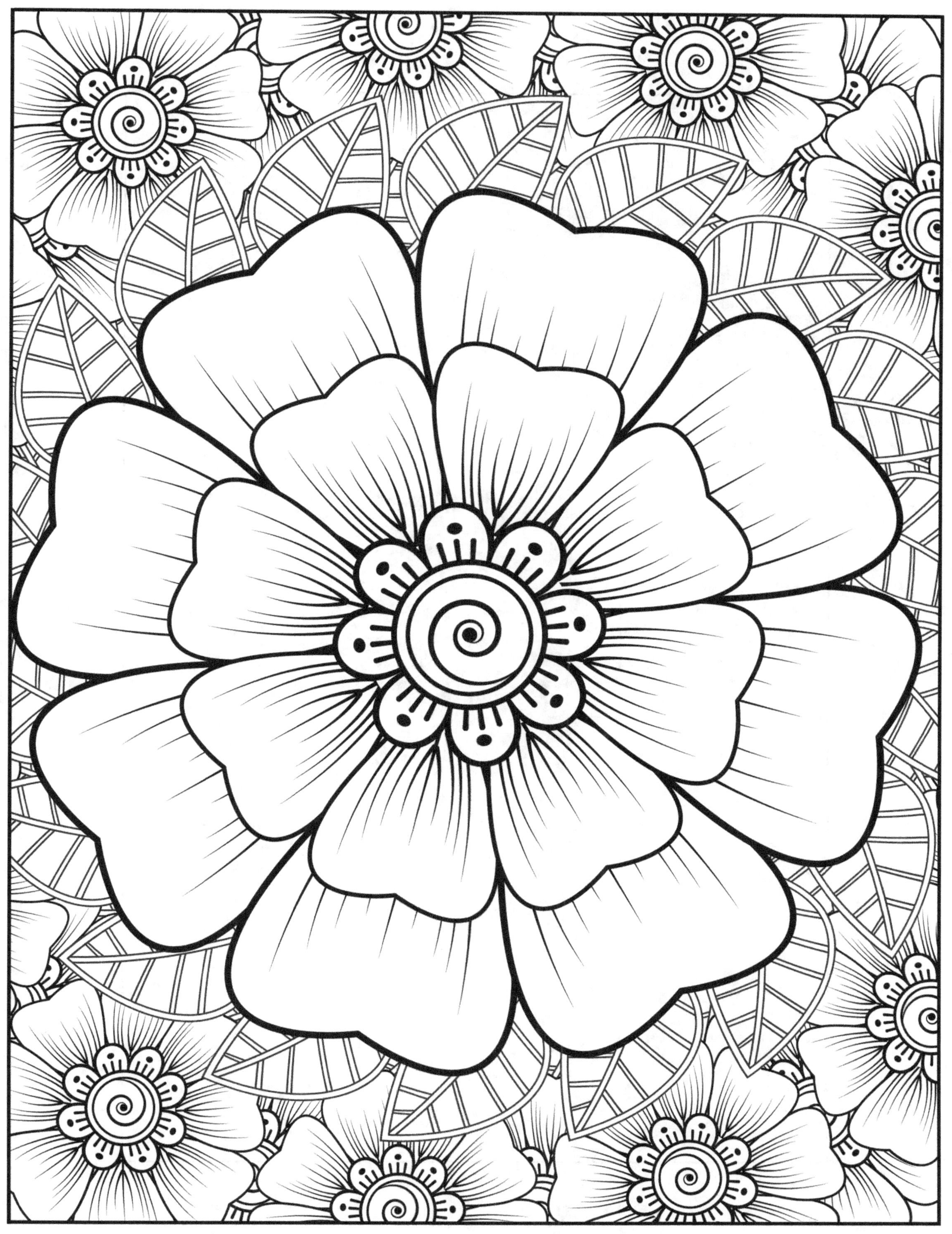

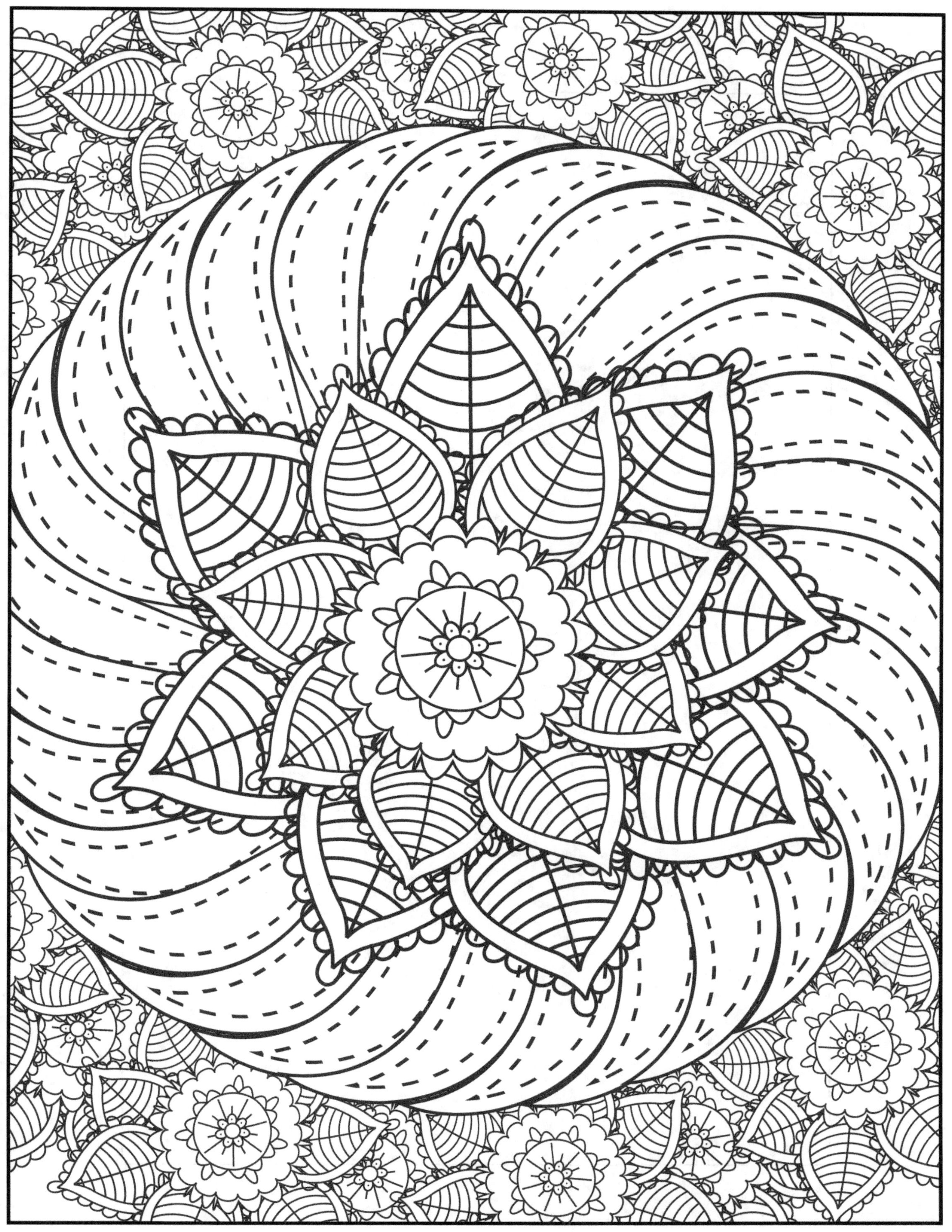

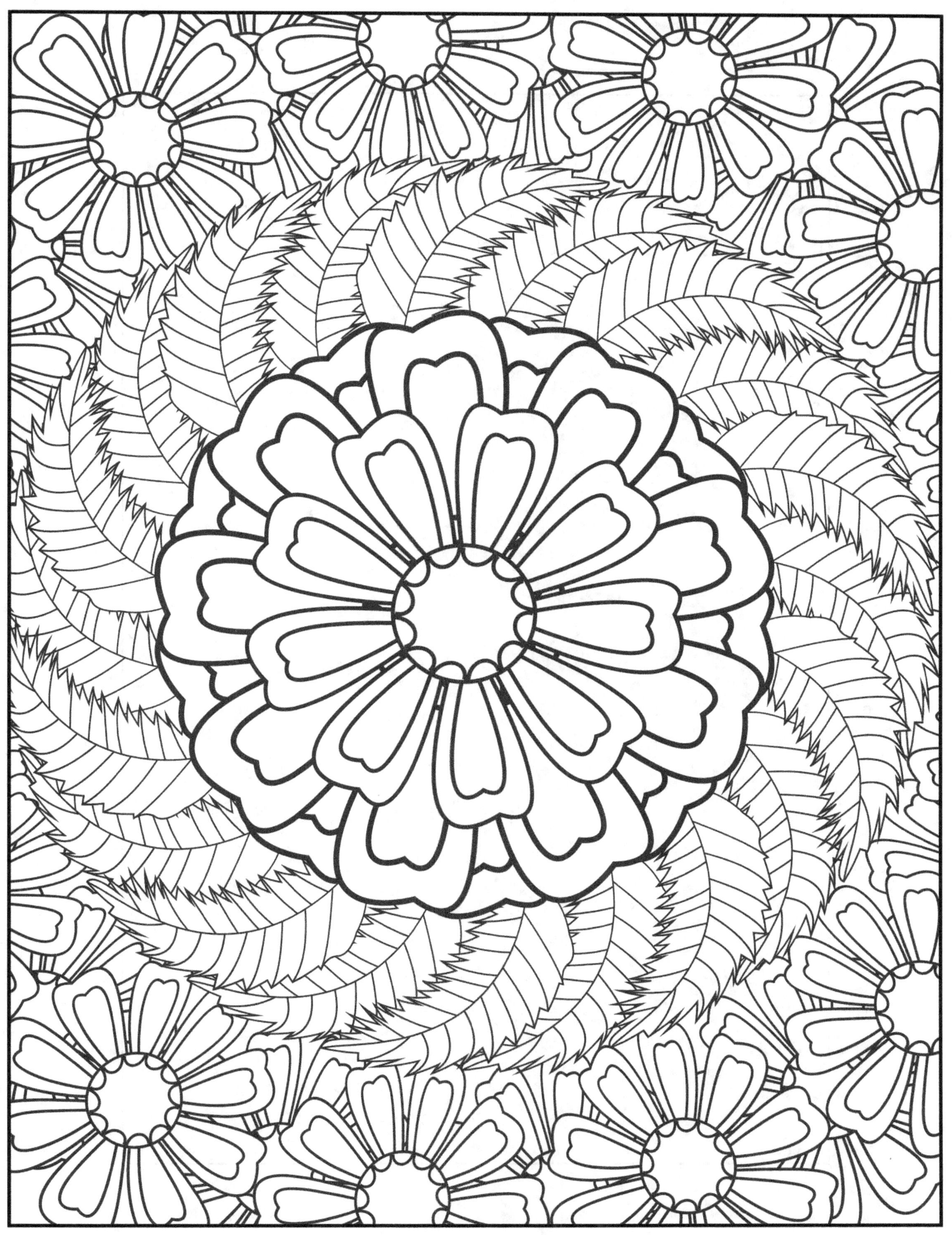

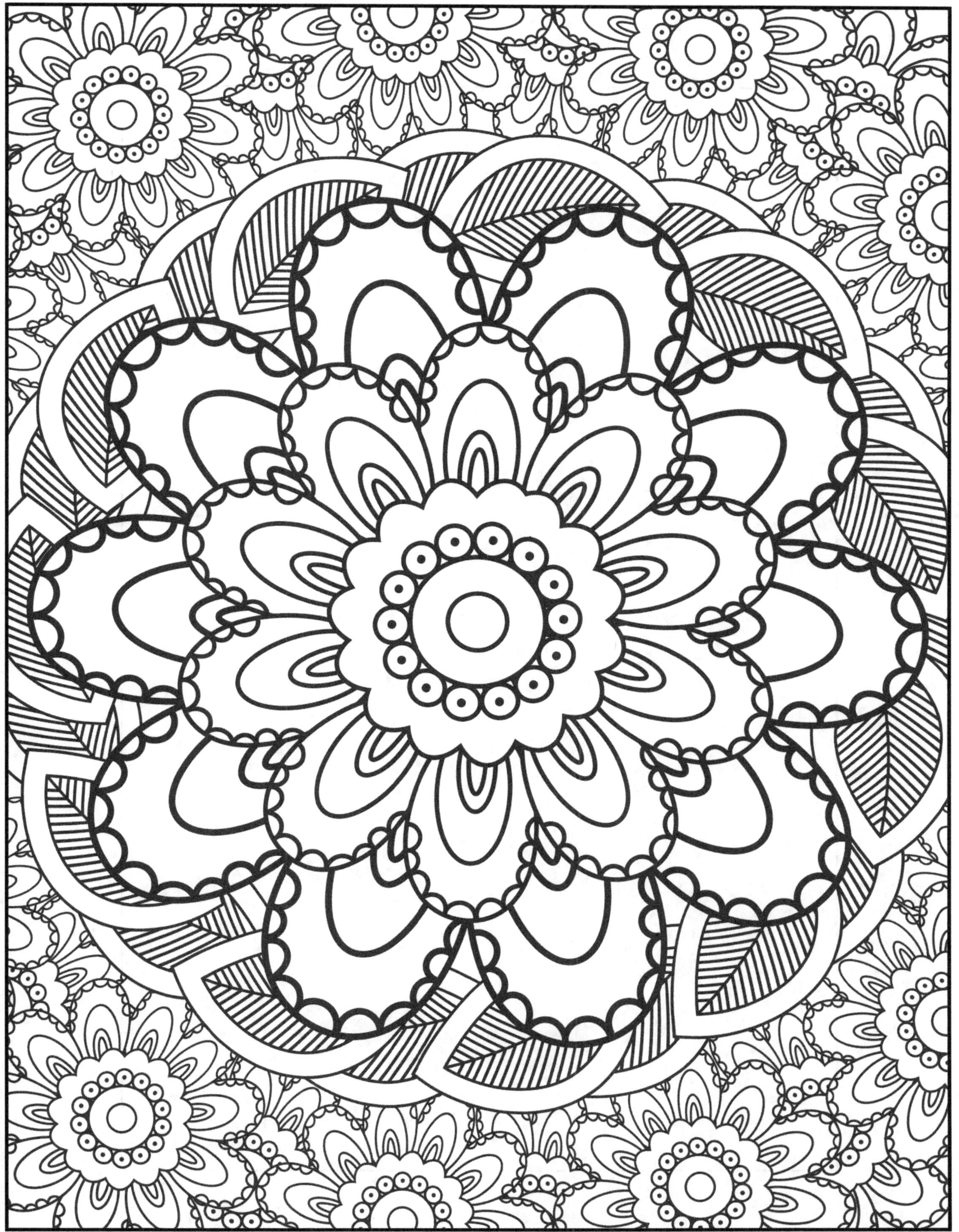

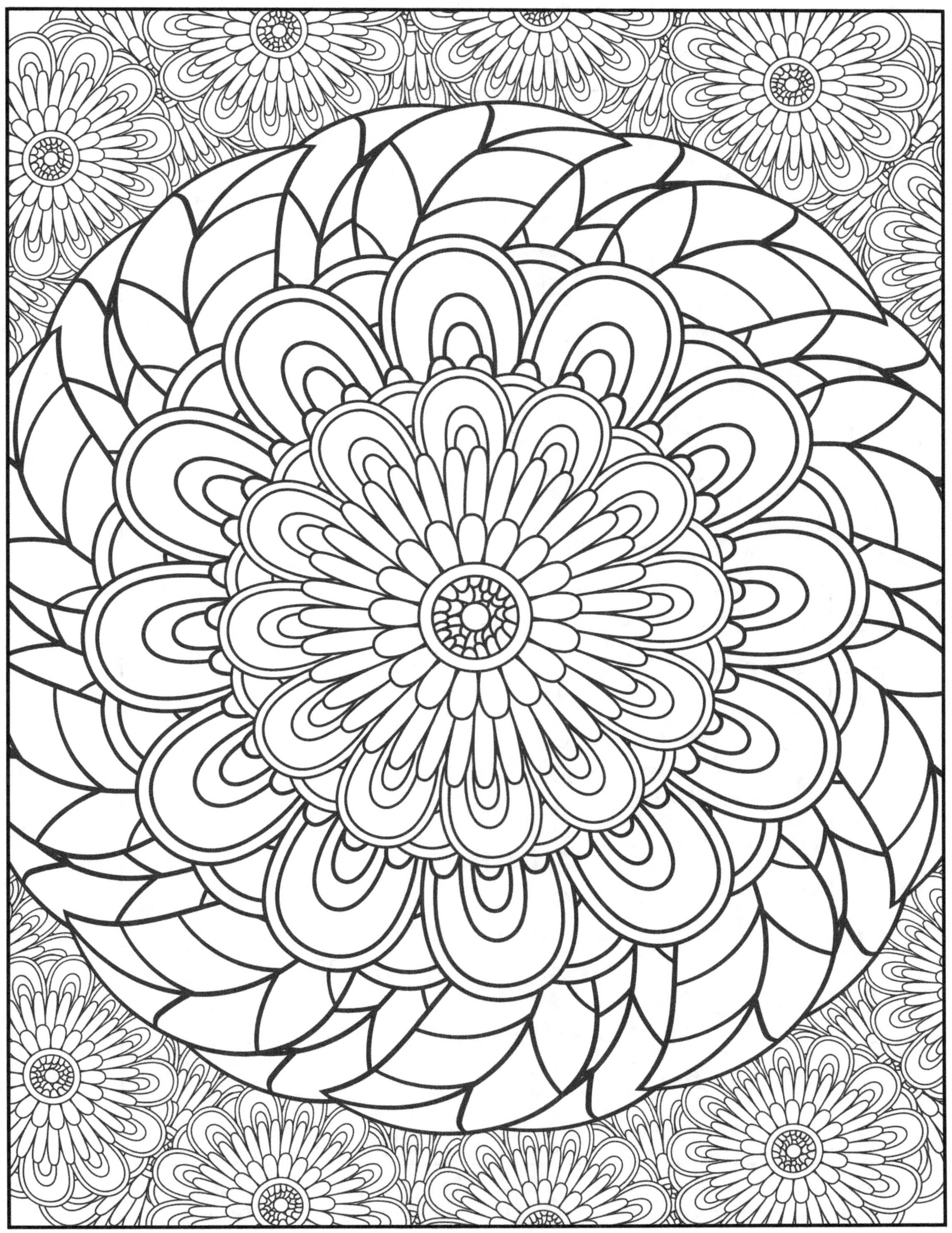

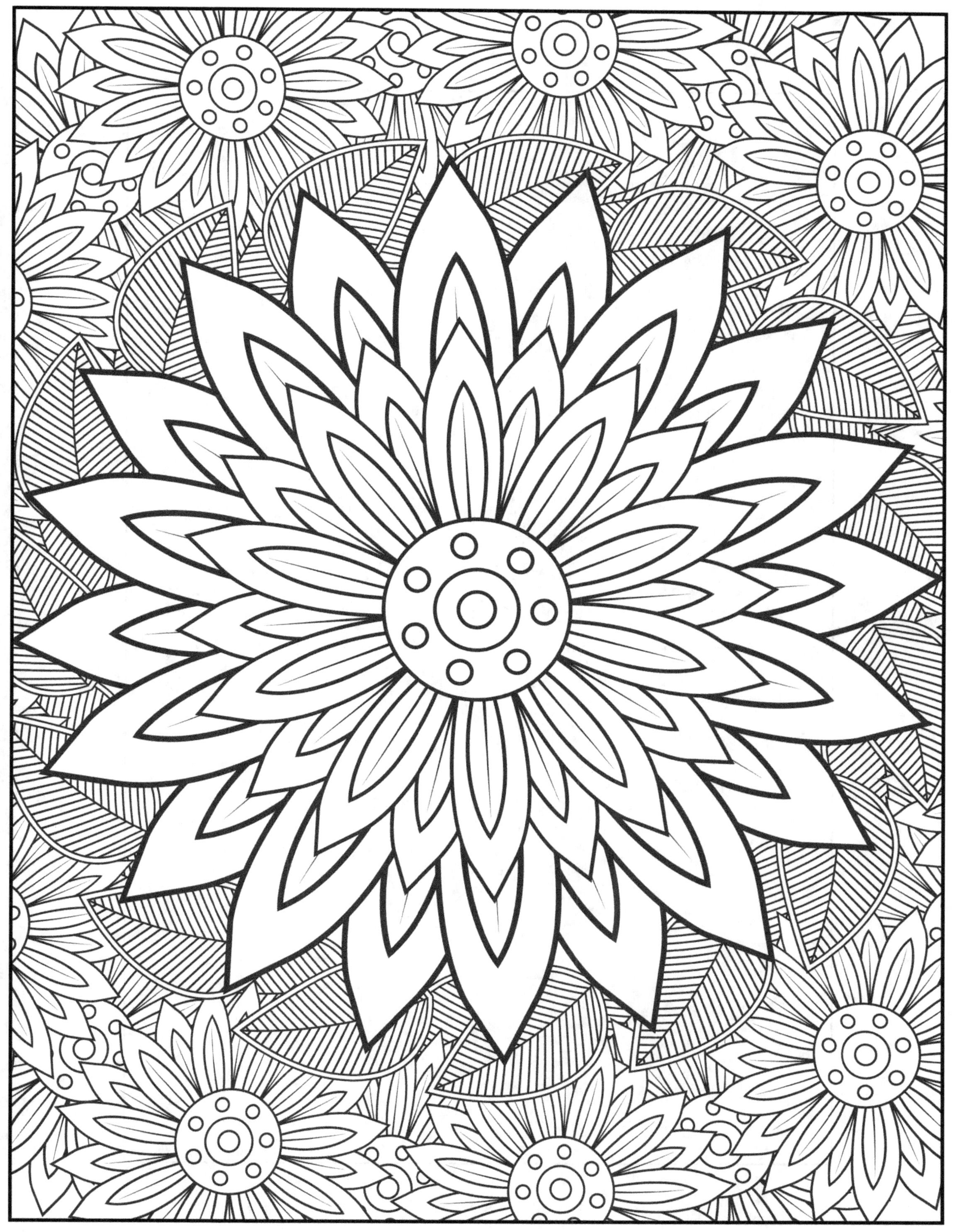

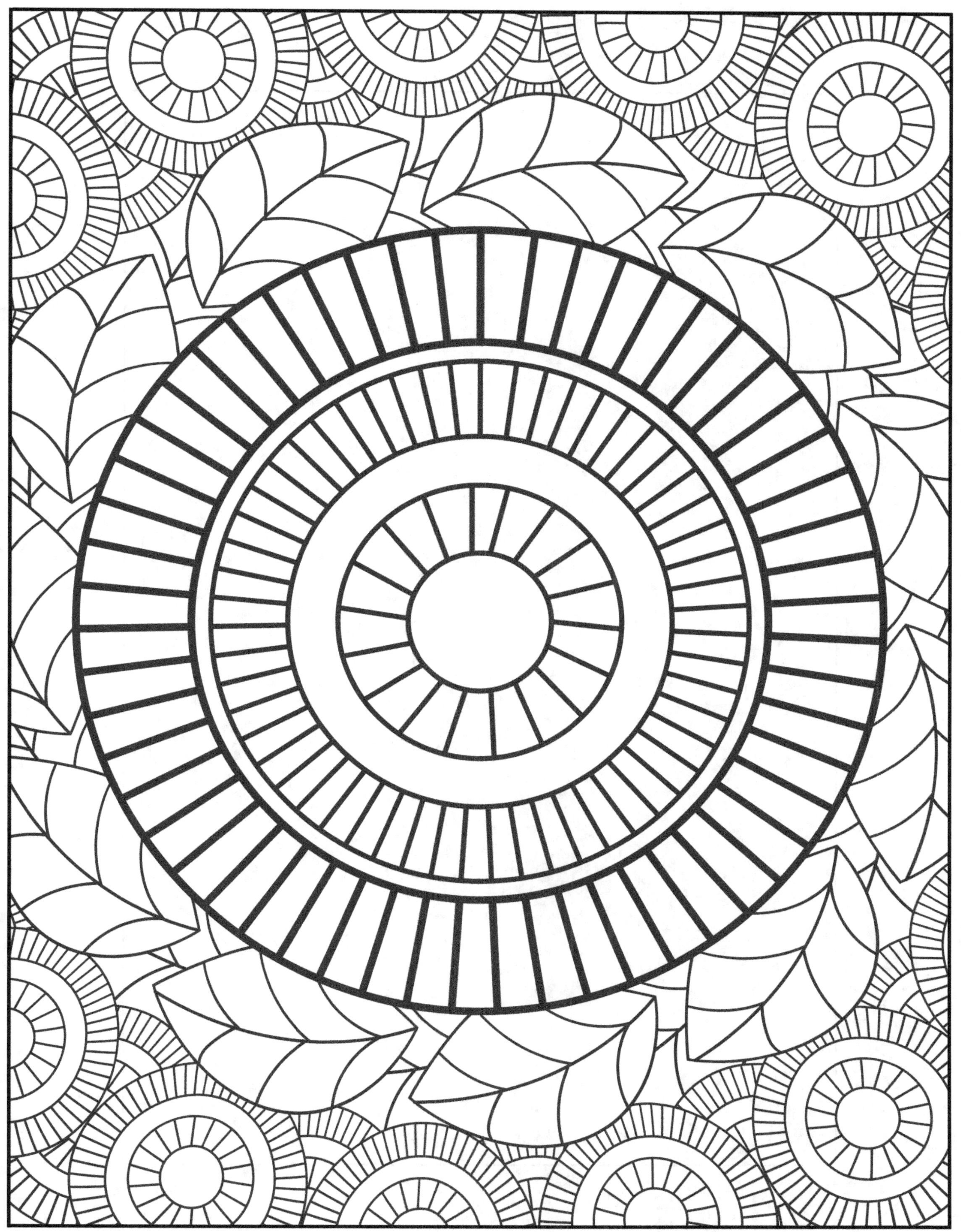

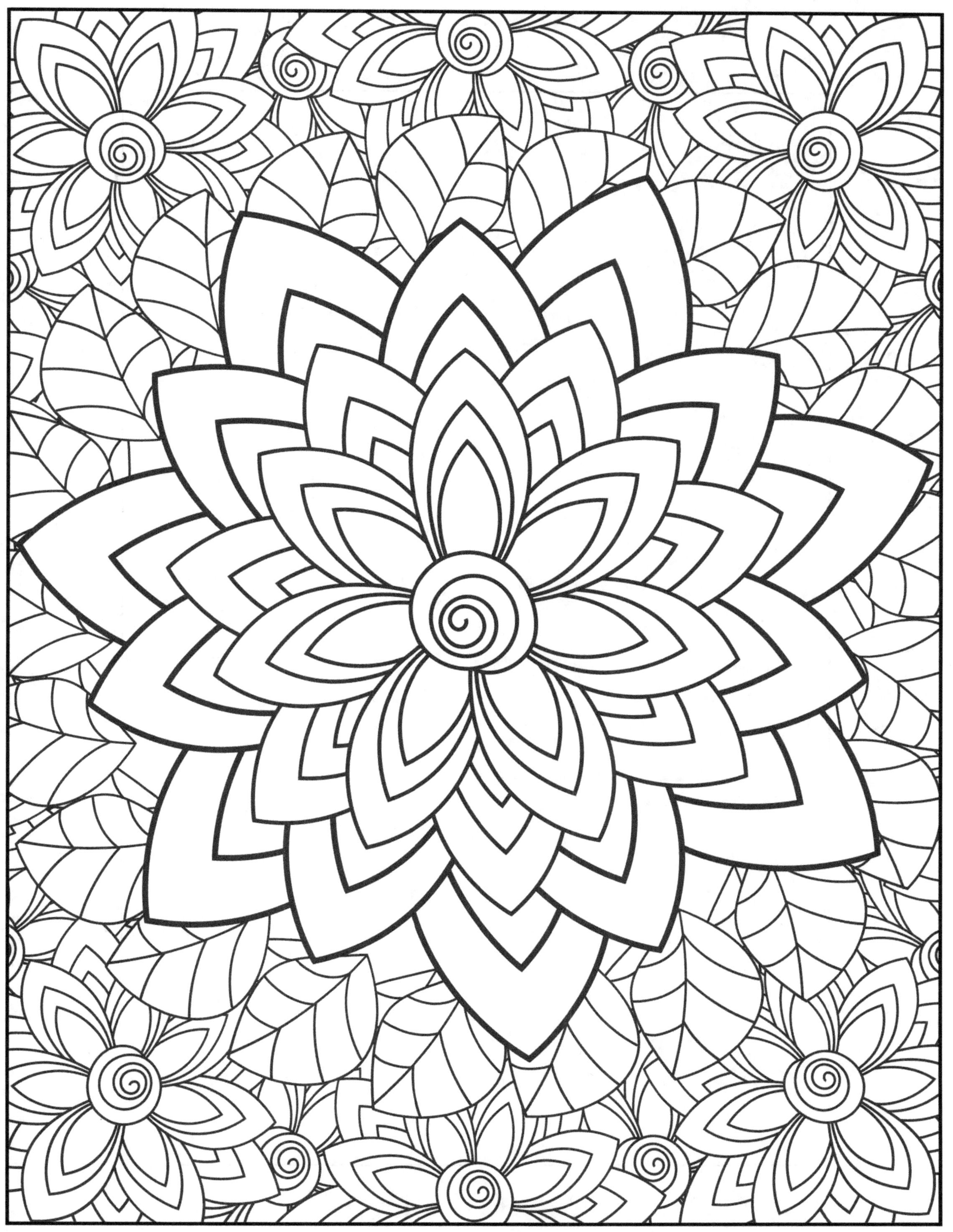

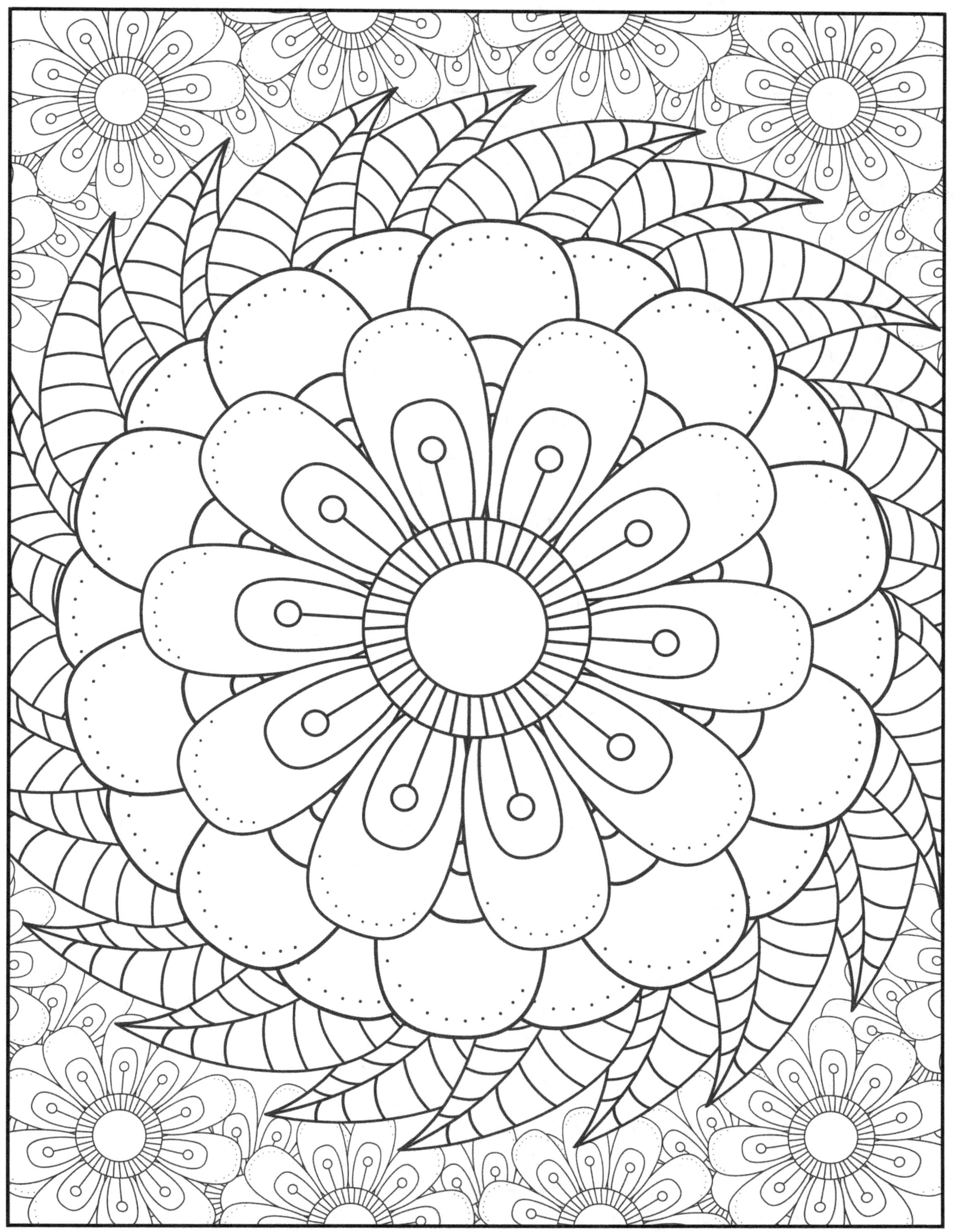

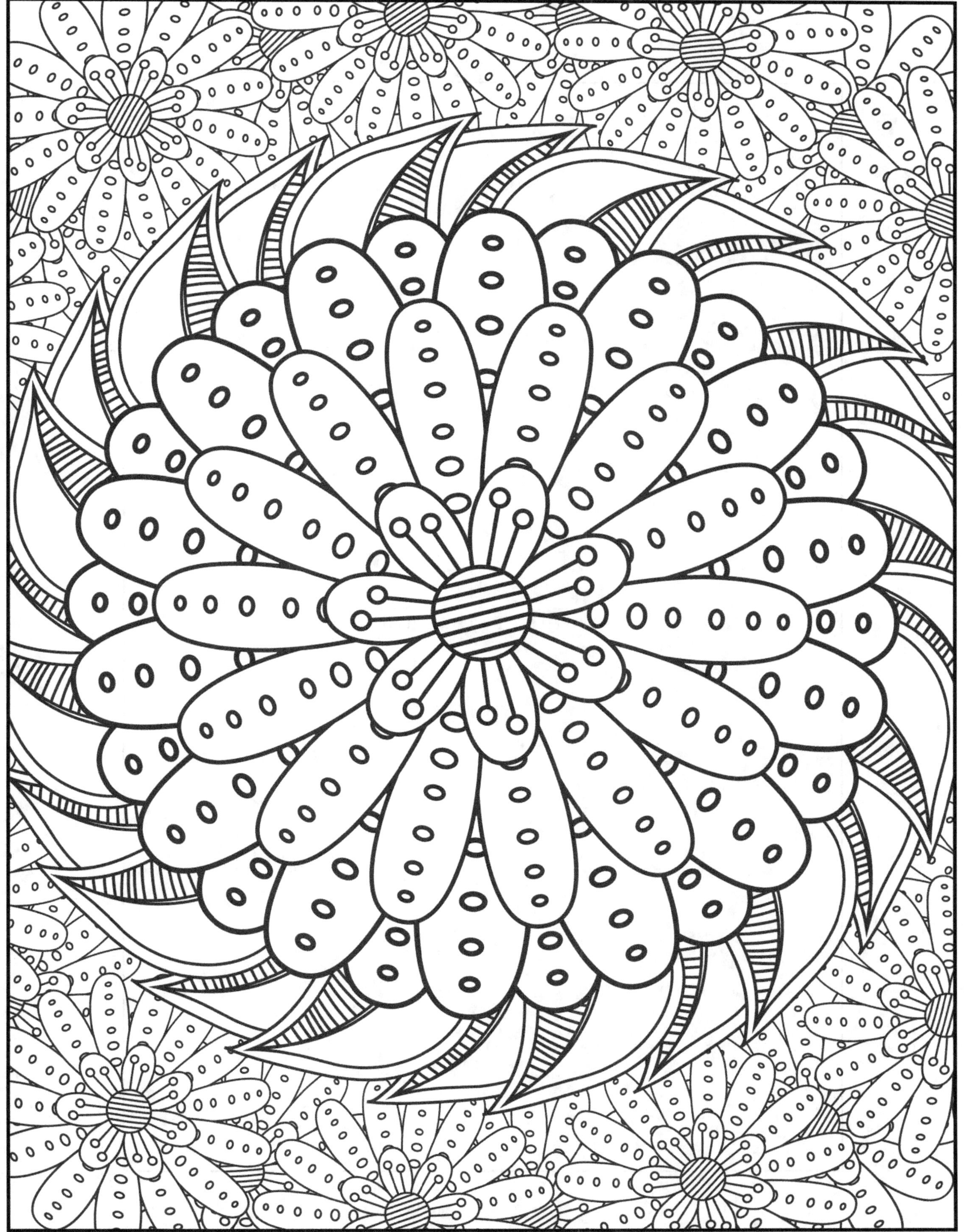

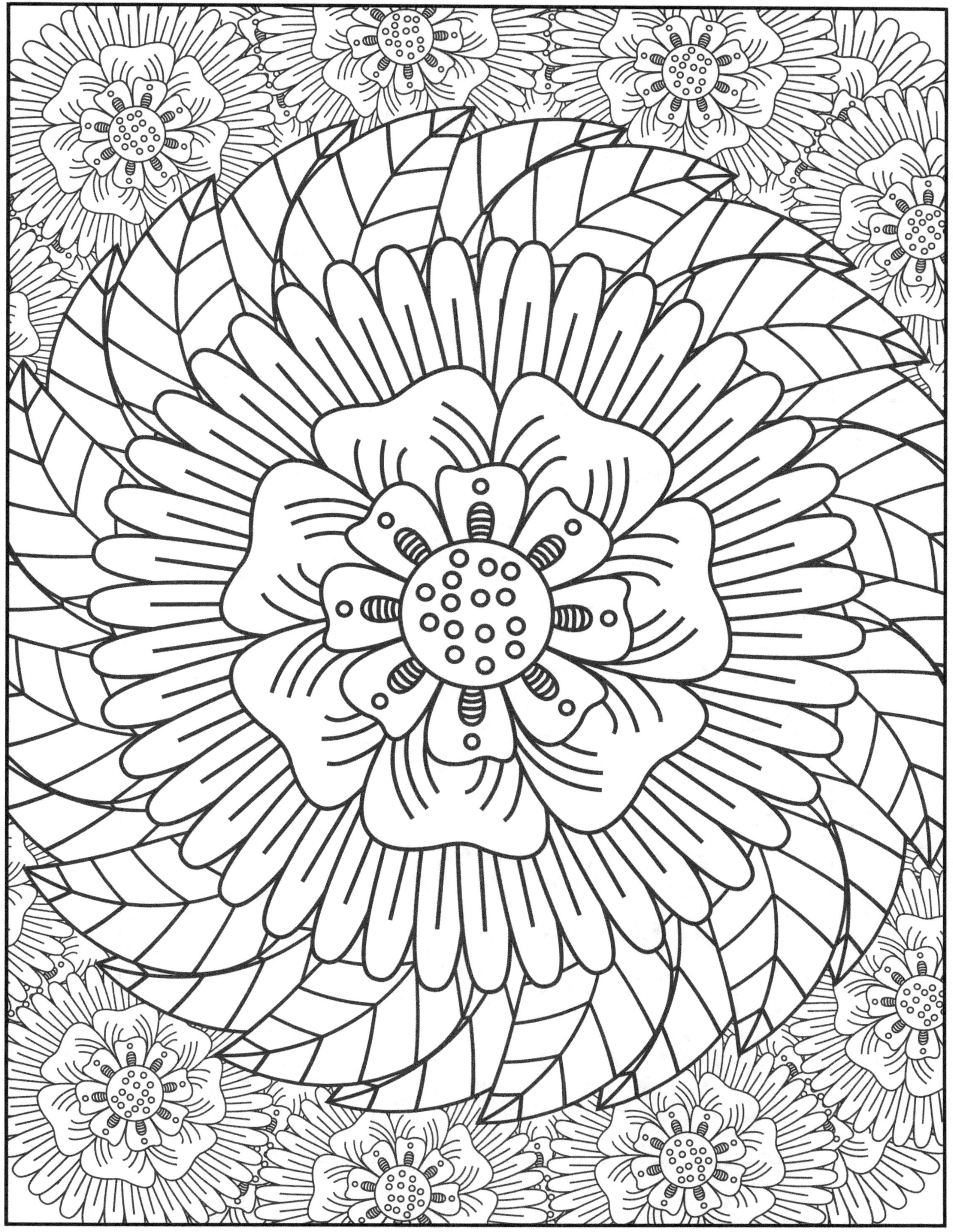

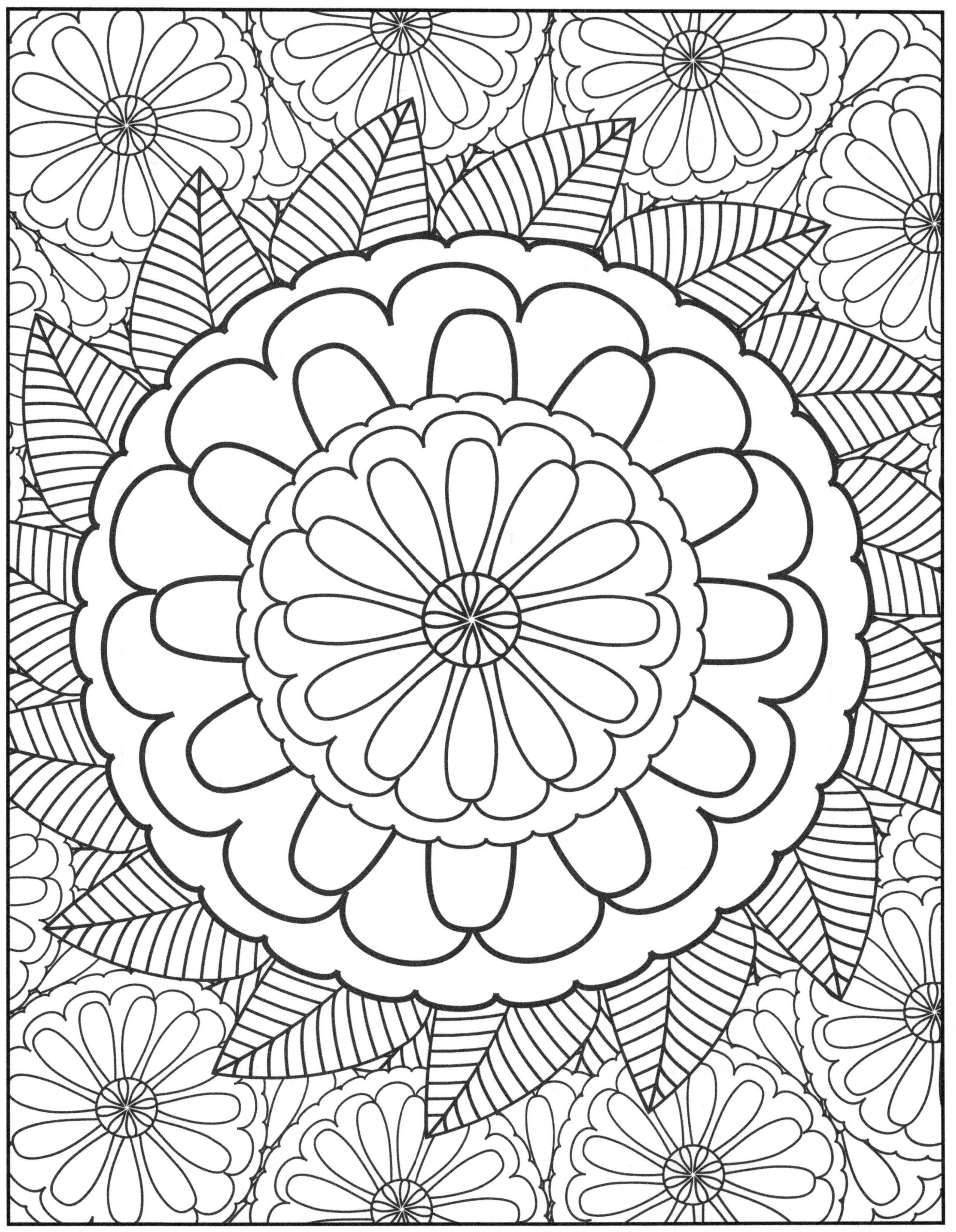

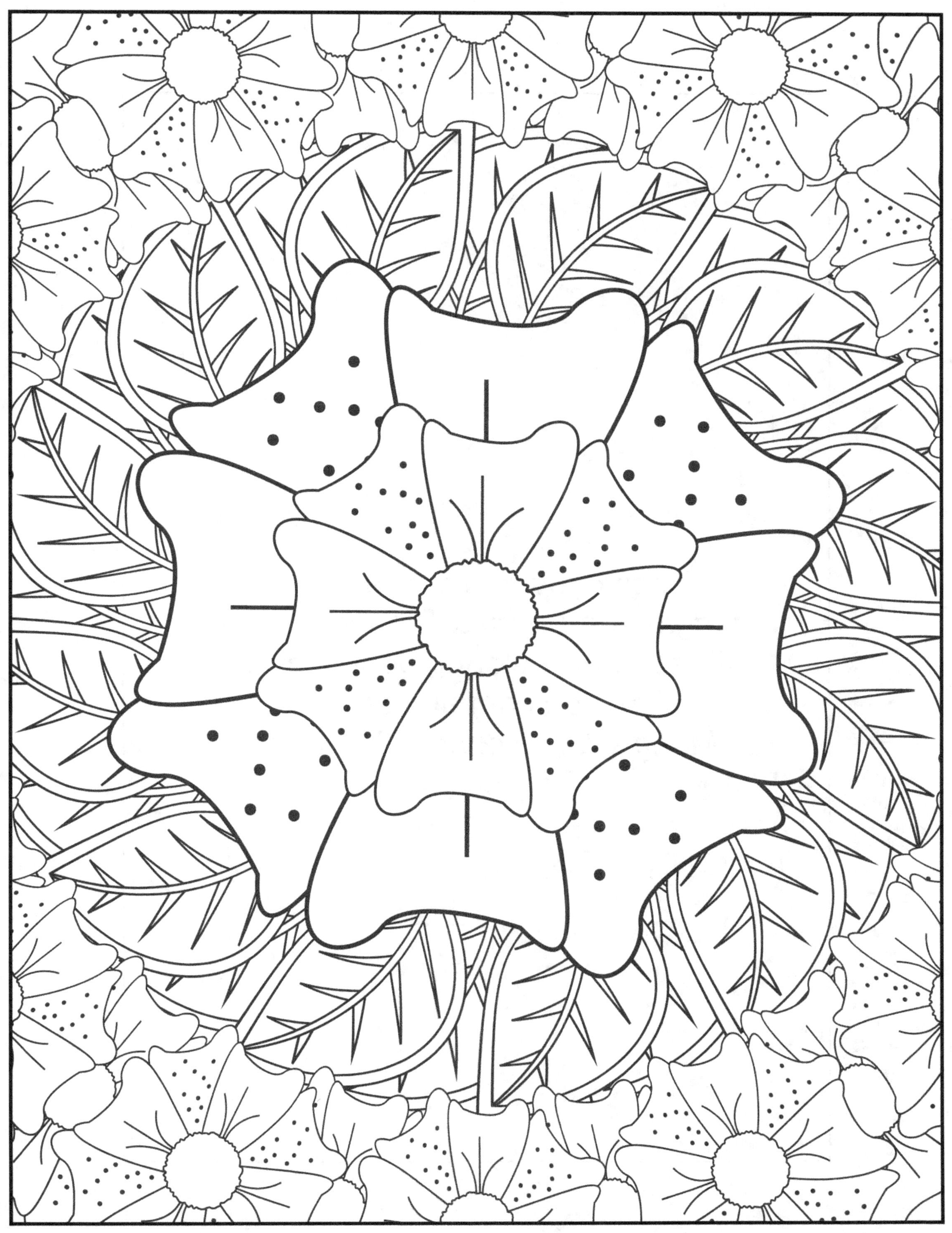

Thank you for purchasing a
Maggie Lee Bennett Creations book.
To see new coloring books, go to
Amazon.com and type in
Maggie Lee Bennett Creations.